Y0-BVQ-902

Growing Parent

A
Sourcebook
for
Families

Growing Parent

A Sourcebook for Families

BY THE EDITORS OF
GROWING CHILD/GROWING PARENT

Contemporary Books, Inc.
Chicago

Library of Congress Cataloging in Publication Data

Main entry under title:

Growing parent, a sourcebook for families.

    1. Parenting.   2. Parenting—Psychological aspects.
I. Growing child.   II. Growing parent.
HQ755.8.G76   1983   649′.1   83-7675
ISBN 0-8092-5486-7

Copyright © 1983 by Dunn & Hargitt, Inc.
All rights reserved
Published by Contemporary Books, Inc.
180 North Michigan Avenue, Chicago, Illinois 60601
Manufactured in the United States of America
Library of Congress Catalog Card Number: 83-7675
International Standard Book Number: 0-8092-5486-7

Published simultaneously in Canada by Beaverbooks, Ltd.
195 Allstate Parkway, Valleywood Business Park
Markham, Ontario L3R 4T8 Canada

Contributors: Jan Allen, Kitty Dubin,
Sharon Epstein, Donald W. Felker,
Evelyn H. Felker, Lynn Holland,
Sandy Jones, Judith Myers-Walls,
Charles Riker, Raymond Schuessler,
Barbara Stein, Burton L. White

Contents

Foreword

Isn't it amazing what changes children bring about in our lives?

At first, when babies are so unbelievably tiny, it's just getting from day to day that's important . . . keeping diapers changed, babies cleaned and fed, making emergency runs to the super-market for food, and trying to arrange for some uninterrupted sleep. It doesn't seem possible for one so small to create so much work.

As the months, then years, go by, somehow we mature (we think) and learn to deal with the Tooth Fairy, chore coopera-tion (good luck!), playmates, broken bones, and eventually school. And all the time we worry about the kind of parents we've become.

Most of the time I think we come up with fifty-fifty results, by our own evaluation: half of the time we're pleased with the way we've handled something; the other half we're not sure we've done the right thing. But basically we're never completely satisfied, and we still keep trying to do better. In short, we try to become still better parents. We talk about what we've done, what we *could* have done, what went wrong. Always analyzing.

Nowadays, of course, there are a great many people who are trying to help us do a better job as parents: physicians, educators, toymakers, publishers, and so on. More than ever before, parents are being inundated with everything from designer rubber pants to music lessons for two-year-olds!

How can parents pick and choose from among the myriad of products, services, and advice and come up with what is exactly right for their family?

Dennis Dunn and the folks at *Growing Child/Growing Parent* believe there are as many parenting styles as there are families . . . that there is no one "perfect" way to do anything. In the process of growing and maturing as a family, *you* make the choices that will eventually determine your parenting style.

In order to make choices, you must first have *information* from which to choose. And the more information you have, the more informed your choices will be.

Over the years I've gotten to know the people at *Growing Child/Growing Parent,* and watched them grow and mature, too, just like a family. They're a very close-knit group of people who believe children and parents are a very special combination that deserves support, encouragement, and nurture. For *Growing Child/Growing Parent* parenting is, indeed, a business. But its primary motivation is not the bottom line on the balance sheet; it is to help provide an environment where kids can grow up to become whole, competent, loving individuals.

Readers have always been able to get back issues of *Growing Child* but not *Growing Parent.* Those requesting copies of their favorite articles found they weren't available. So, putting those articles together in one book as "the best of *Growing Parent*" seemed to be a good idea.

There are topics here that you'll rarely find addressed elsewhere, either in books or magazine articles, all written with a down-to-earth approach and lots of the "how-tos" we all love. These articles help you feel positive and worthwhile as a parent and as a spouse.

Over the years the folks at *Growing Child/Growing Parent*

and I have shared ideas, opinions, and tips back and forth—after all, we're in the same business—and to some extent we also share the same philosophy about information for parents.

How *can* parents pick and choose from all the information available today and come up with what is exactly right for your family?

1. Be informed.
2. Don't believe everything you see, hear, or read.
3. Examine the options.
4. Trust your instincts.
5. Always ask questions.

This book is a good place to start looking, reading, and asking questions about your role as parents.

Vicki Lansky

Vicki Lansky
Publisher/editor of "Practical Parenting Newsletter"
Author of: *Feed Me, I'm Yours*
The Taming of the C.A.N.D.Y. Monster
Practical Parenting Tips
Dear Babysitter

Growing Parent

A Sourcebook for Families

Becoming a More Self-Confident Parent

Being a parent is a tremendous responsibility.

Parents are expected to feed and clothe tiny, helpless human beings, to teach them to get along in the world, and to encourage them to like themselves and others. These many responsibilities often lead parents to question themselves and their abilities.

A person might ask, "Was I really ready to become a parent?" or, "Do I know enough about children?" or, "What have I gotten myself into?"

Such anxieties and insecurities are common. The most disturbing thing about these worries is that they can get worse as parents learn more about children. The more you know, the more you know about what can go wrong!

Anxieties and insecurities about parenting are often related to low self-confidence and low self-esteem. Low self-confidence can act as handcuffs, holding parents back. They become so worried about doing something wrong that they do almost nothing with the child, even though they would be very good parents if they tried.

Parents who are so handicapped by anxiety that they can do nothing are rare. But small anxieties can chip away at parents' self-confidence and affect their ability to interact with their children. Therefore, one of the most important things parents can do is build their own self-confidence.

This building up often happens naturally with the passage of time and the gaining of experience. Parents find that many of their worries were unnecessary, and they discover that they actually can do some good parenting. There are also some special techniques parents can use to raise their self-confidence and help their partners raise theirs without waiting around, hoping experience will do the trick.

FIVE KEYS TO POSITIVE PARENTING SELF-CONCEPT

There are five keys to improving parenting self-concepts:

1. Praise yourself.
2. Evaluate realistically.
3. Set reasonable goals.
4. Encourage your spouse to praise himself or herself.
5. Learn to praise others.

Praise Yourself

Although praising yourself is the most basic of the five keys to positive parenting, it is in some ways also the most difficult to practice. Many individuals are afraid of praising themselves because they think that pride will get the best of them. However, there are two reasons why this is unlikely.

First, if you praise yourself more than you deserve, someone will surely speak up and point out your shortcomings. Second, your upbringing in this society has probably taught you to be very uncomfortable with praising yourself too much. Either you or those around you will keep your self-praise under control.

When you do something well you probably say something nice to yourself, but it is likely that you say it silently. It is important to teach yourself to say those positive things out loud. Tell yourself exactly what you did well and what was good about it.

Begin with specific acts and then move on to more general personal qualities. To protect yourself from some of the skeptics around you, stress how you feel rather than how good something is according to some subjective standard.

For example, you might tell your spouse, "I feel good about the way I handled Johnny after he broke that vase. I let him know I was really upset without losing my temper completely." Your spouse may disagree with the way you handled the situation, but he or she cannot disagree that you feel good about it.

There may be several positive results when you learn to praise yourself. First, when you learn to praise yourself you are able to give yourself rewards when others do not notice or recognize the special things you have done. Second, if you learn to point out to yourself the ways that you are a good parent, you may begin to realize that you can do things pretty effectively after all. This positive parenting self-concept not only encourages you, but it also can make you a better parent because you believe in what you are doing.

Evaluate Realistically

The first principle of realistic evaluations is not to expect yourself to be perfect. The picture of a "perfect parent"—one who is always kind, patient, loving, intelligent, in control, and so on—is impossible to fulfill, and it may not be so perfect in the first place. For example, parents who are always patient may not be preparing their children for a world full of impatient people.

Failure is difficult enough to deal with when it is real. But trying to be perfect is simply inviting unnecessary failure. The important thing is not perfect behavior at all times, but growth toward increased competence.

A second factor in realistic self-evaluation is to compare your behavior as a parent to your own past performance rather than to some other person's parenting. Instead of feeling like a failure because you did not spend three hours a night working or playing with your kids like the father next door, praise yourself for spending a half hour more with them this week than you did last week.

Finally, be specific about your self-evaluation. If you try a new method of discipline for a week and it fails miserably, do not simply decide that you are a failure as a parent. Tell yourself that you did a good job of sticking to the new plan or that you are a pretty good parent for caring enough to try something new, even though it did not work. Make your failure easier to accept by praising your success.

Set Reasonable Goals

Reasonable goals have these characteristics:

1. They are individualized.

2. They are made in relation to past performance.
3. They are attainable through a series of small, manageable steps.

Individualized goals are those you set for yourself. Decide which goal is important to you and how you want to reach that goal.

Setting goals in relation to past performance means that you will be building on your strengths and trying to make improvements that are possible for you.

Finally, having a goal that is attainable through a series of small steps makes the goal seem more manageable. If your goal is encouraging your child to go to college, for instance, helping with homework once a week might eventually lead to your overall goal.

Encourage Your Spouse to Praise Himself or Herself

This suggestion is closely related to the first one: praise yourself. If your spouse praises himself or herself, he or she will get the same benefits.

Our society does not seem to approve of people telling themselves that they have done something well. That is why it is important to encourage your spouse. If you support each other in this way, it will be much easier for both of you to be encouraged.

If your spouse finds it difficult to say good things about himself or herself, you may need to help a little. Point out when your spouse has done things well as a parent and say, "You were really patient with the baby tonight. You should give yourself a gold star!"

Learn to Praise Others

Some people fear that praising themselves is dangerous because they will get so involved in themselves that they will forget others. It does not work that way. Praise multiplies. Learning to praise yourself helps you learn to praise others, and praising others often brings you praise in return. You will find yourself looking for positive things rather than concentrating on negative things or weaknesses.

LEARNING TO ACCEPT PRAISE

Another skill you may need to learn is how to accept praise. Many of us respond to a compliment by denying it, insisting that we are not worthy of the praise. Instead, try saying, "Thank you" and saying something nice (and sincere) in return.

These five keys are a system to help parents develop and maintain a more positive self-concept. Try them and see if you are more encouraged. Then give yourself a pat on the back for caring enough about parenting to read this book in order to improve your skill.

When They Won't Stop Crying, or First Aid for Fussy Babies

A young mother expresses the anguish many mothers feel with a continually crying or "colicky" baby when she says, "I thought I was going to sail through living with a second baby using experience." I want to say that colic is not caused by nervous mothers—colic is real, colic is pain.

She is one of thousands of new mothers each year who have a less than happy baby. Fussiness is an extremely common problem in infants. Recent studies show that most babies have fussy periods once a day lasting from half an hour to four or five hours. One out of four babies has periods of crying that last more than three hours a day and occur more than three days a week.

There are real differences in fussy babies. Some are mild complainers, while others scream and seem to be in real agony. Some can't stand to be moved or even touched, while others want to be held all the time. In both cases there are definite strategies that parents can use to help their babies and themselves. Medical research, too, is uncovering new clues about what's causing baby's discomfort.

COLIC versus FUSSING

Fussing and *colic* are words that are often used interchangeably to describe a baby's crying. Sometimes it's difficult to determine whether your baby has colic or is simply fussier than most babies.

All babies seem to have times when they need to let off steam. For most babies this period of fussiness is in the evening.

Some babies are good self-soothers and go to sleep best when they've had a few minutes to cry off tension before settling down. Other babies lose control when they cry and only cry harder and harder when they're left alone. How well a baby can soothe himself from crying seems to be built in at birth.

THE OVERREACTING BABY

The strategy that you adopt to soothe your fussy baby will depend a lot on the baby's own characteristics. Not all babies are alike. Some become unglued at the least disturbance—a sudden noise, a change in temperature, or an abrupt motion—while other babies positively demand to be actively stimulated.

Many times overreacting or "skin sensitive" babies are premature babies who have spent long periods of time in an incubator. Perhaps their nervous systems have not developed to the point that they can integrate the noise and confusion of the outside world, or perhaps they are simply resistant to change from their accustomed isolation. Here are some helpful coping tips:

Swaddling

Swaddling is the age-old practice of wrapping a baby firmly in a blanket or onto a flat cradleboard. Swaddling appears to soothe a distraught baby by restraining movement, which, in turn, signals the baby's brain to shut down for sleep. Care must be taken to avoid binding the baby too tightly and to allow the baby adequate time for exploration and free movement when he's not fussy.

Pacification

Sometimes a pacifier, a bottle nipple, or extra time at the breast can soothe an irritable baby. Many babies learned hand and finger sucking before birth but may need to relearn the skill because of the changes in body weight and the pull of gravity after birth.

Temperature Control

Many small babies are sensitive to changes in temperature and humidity. Young babies have only very primitive mechanisms for dealing with cold or heat. Often they cry when they are uncomfortable.

If diapering and bathing cause your baby to shudder and cry, try damp-mopping him with a warm washcloth while he remains covered by a warm blanket. Placing the baby across your lap on a hot water bottle filled with lukewarm water can help, too, as can warm mittens and booties.

Soothing Sounds

Tiny microphones placed inside the uterus before birth have picked up many sounds, including the droning and pulsing noises from the veins and arteries feeding the placenta. Tape recordings of these sounds can have a remarkably soothing effect in the early months after birth.

Other monotonous, droning sounds often work just as well in soothing a baby. Some mothers have found that vacuum cleaner noises or recordings of dishwasher sounds work temporarily, as does the soothing sound of an aquarium pump. An expensive stuffed teddy bear is also available that has womb sounds recorded in its belly.

The Colic Carry

When baby is having a crying attack, some parents have found that placing her face down across one of their arms, so that the baby's cheek is at the adult's elbow crease, can help ease the baby's abdominal pressure. The hand of the same arm

is used to grasp the baby's leg or thigh. The baby is then jiggled or rocked gently up and down while the other hand is used to gently massage the baby's belly.

Two other quick actions that may help interrupt a baby's crying jag are to lift her up and down in very wide arcs, almost to the point of deep knee bends, and actually imitate the baby's own crying sounds, which may work because it startles the baby. One researcher has found that tape recording the baby's own cries and playing them back can bring crying to an abrupt halt.

Controlled Motion

Often a fussy baby has little tolerance for movement, so parents must learn to slow down handling motions. Try talking, gesturing, and moving in a more studied and calm way.

A baby who reacts strongly to sounds and other outside stimuli will also react to the tension that he feels in your arms and your rapid breathing when you are upset. The secret is to allow your muscles to soften as you practice deliberate, deep breaths, similar to the dynamic relaxation taught in childbirth education classes, particularly during feeding.

THE DEMANDING BABY

On the opposite pole to the baby who cries at the slightest disturbance is the baby who demands constant stimulation in order not to cry. This baby wants to be held . . . and held . . . and held. The following suggestions may prove helpful.

A Baby Carrier

A soft fabric baby carrier that straps baby to you can be an excellent soothing device. Maybe your vociferous baby is demanding the intimacy and frequent feedings that are the human tradition. Studies of the milk composition of humans in comparison to animals show that babies were probably meant to be carried continuously and fed very frequently.

Rocking

Granny's rocking chair still has a place in the bedroom or kitchen of modern homes. Studies have shown that rocking not only soothes irritable babies; it may also contribute to their motor development by stimulating an inner ear organ responsible for balance and coordination.

More than one mother has labeled her automatic baby swing as her "supper saver" because it soothes baby long enough for the family to eat. Most babies tend to be their fussiest in the early evening hours. If you decide to purchase a swing, look for one that has the longest windup time, and use a restraining belt to prevent baby from flopping forward.

COLIC

Colic is a catchall word applied to babies who cry night and day. While a fussy baby complains and protests, especially when tired or hungry, a colicky baby wakes up crying during the night and spends the day coming in and out of desperate screams that seem to be triggered by eating or by some inner pain signal.

About 3 percent of all babies suffer from severe colic. Here's how Dr. Emelyn Coolidge described a severe colic attack in a baby book in 1914, *Home Care of Sick Children:*

> The baby with colic screams lustily and in paroxyms. His face is first red, but may become pale or even blue around the mouth if the attacks last long and are severe. The hands and feet are cold, the legs are drawn up, the abdomen as a rule is very hard and distended, and the baby works his hands in agony.

Does that sound like your baby?

Unfortunately, there's no quick and easy explanation for why your baby has colic and cries so much. Scientists still are unable to pinpoint the exact physical causes of many cases of colic in babies.

One couple I know found that their baby's sudden, extreme

bouts of crying were caused by a hiatal hernia that had not been diagnosed earlier. Sometimes physicians discover that male babies are crying because of a hernia in the scrotum area. In both cases parents observed that the hernia area became hot and distended during crying.

Sometimes cow milk proteins can cause an allergic reaction in the mother that is then transferred through her milk to her baby. In a Swedish study of nineteen colicky babies who were breast-fed, three-fourths were "cured" when their mothers rigidly followed a cow's milk-free diet. If you find that you don't like to drink milk yourself, it may be because you are allergic to it.

Cow's milk formulas can also account for intense allergic reactions in allergy-prone babies. Iron in baby vitamins or formulas may also be the culprit, causing baby to have belly pain and green, watery diarrhea. Be sure to check with your doctor, though, before changing vitamins or formula.

Some forms of colic may actually be caused by a urinary tract infection or other urinary problems in babies. But sometimes physicians are hesitant to attempt urinalysis with young babies because usable specimens are difficult to gather. In some cases urinary infections in babies fail to show up except with more sophisticated tests such as leukocyte counts and a blood urea nitrogen (BUN) test.

Another possible cause of undiagnosed pain and crying in babies may be related to an immature or malfunctioning esophagus. The baby's esophagus serves two important roles. One is to carry air-free milk from the baby's mouth to his stomach, and the other is to keep gastric juices from coming back up into the baby's mouth. If the squeezing of the esophagus is off rhythm, or parts of the esophagus are too small and tight, then air swallowing is increased, and discomfort and digestive disorders may result.

Some physicians prescribe sedatives for colicky babies to make them drowsy so that they sleep—a practice that may give parents temporary relief but may also have serious side effects for the baby. These can include undesirable central nervous system depression, restlessness, stomach and intestinal disturbances, dry mouth, loss of appetite, and constipation.

MEETING YOUR OWN NEEDS

The psychological effects of having a fussy or colicky baby are profound for parents. Besides their obvious physical exhaustion from lack of sleep, many parents experience a state of crisis that affects not only their own sense of well-being but also their relationship with one another. Often mothers feel guilty for their babies' discontent—a feeling that is reinforced by physicians who cling to older "tense mother, tense baby" theories and by relatives who warn parents against "spoiling" the baby because they respond to his cries.

Many mothers find themselves "out of synch" with other mothers who have content, sleep-through-the-night babies. The barrage of negative feedback and crying from their babies, coupled with isolation from the mothering culture that forms a crucial support system in today's society, leaves many of these mothers in a state of emotional bankruptcy marked by periods of depression, rage, and deeply felt loneliness.

Many parents of fussy babies are finding help through parent-baby support groups where mothers and fathers are free to examine openly their negative feelings. Other parents, too, are good sources for coping advice.

Support groups can be found in universities with early childhood education departments, in churches, and through nonprofit organizations.

The following coping tips come from mothers of fussy babies and parent-baby focus groups.

1. *Sleep when the baby does.* Don't work while the baby sleeps, even during the day. Signal your body that it is time to rest by taking off your clothes, unplugging the telephone, pulling down the shades, and getting under the covers just as you would at night. Minirests wherever you find yourself—on the kitchen floor, on the living room carpet—can work wonders in the midst of a fatiguing day.

2. *Feed yourself like an athlete in training.* Many parents of fussy babies suffer from dietary self-neglect. Eat more protein-rich foods such as meats, cheeses, and legumes. Vitamin and mineral needs are increased, so a supplement

may be in order along with a selection of vitamin-rich vegetables and fruits.

The basic rule of thumb for maximizing the food value of vegetables is to eat them raw when you can, frozen as a second choice, and canned only when the other two options are not available. Preplan meals by cooking larger than usual quantities for freezing and by preparing dinner in the morning when your baby is less likely to be fussy.

3. *Find someone to help you with the housework.* Nothing adds to depression more than the sight of an accumulation of unfinished household tasks. Try calling the guidance counselor at a nearby high school for the names of students seeking part-time work or post an ad seeking help in the local library, grocery store, or senior citizens' center. Part-time cleaning can cost as little as $10 a session and is well worth the price for the peace of mind it brings.

4. *Try not to keep a mental tally against the baby.* Face the fact that having a fussy baby is a "no win" situation. Your baby desperately needs you to be on her side. It is difficult to overlook the stress the baby causes you, but many parents of fussy babies have found that things became easier for them when they yielded to their babies' demands rather than keeping an angry tally of the number of times their babies had cried or awakened during the night.

One simple, yet effective, gesture is to turn the bedroom clock to the wall so that you are not constantly reminded of how little time has elapsed since the baby was last awake. Letting the baby cry it out, a popular practice, does not usually dampen the fussy baby's crying. Not responding may cause even more demands in the months to come.

5. *Try to keep the proper perspective.* Research is showing that most fussy babies gain weight, grow taller, and generally thrive in spite of their discomfort.

Colic is no respecter of persons—it crosses all socioeconomic lines and is just as likely to occur in a family that already has five children as in a family with its first baby. Boys are just as apt to suffer from colic as girls are. It is, however, less common in nonwhite families.

Most colicky babies turn out to be calm, happy preschoolers, and many are brighter than normal, perhaps because of the tremendous amount of parental stimulation they received in their early months.

One reassuring message from parents who've been through it is to remember that in a few months you'll be able to do the things you're not able to do now. And your fretful, fussy baby will be replaced by a lovable, happy little individual.

Is There Intimacy After Parenthood?

Have you ever watched a couple who are listening intently to one another and seem oblivious to the rest of the world?

They laugh, hold hands, and appear relaxed and intimate with each other. It's easier to imagine them as lovers than as parents who are having an evening away from their children.

Intimacy and parenthood are often in conflict. When men and women marry and become parents they gradually begin to trade in parts of themselves that are spontaneous, communicative, fun-loving, and sexual in exchange for attitudes more "appropriate" to the serious and demanding roles they are assuming as "Mother" and "Father."

THE TRADITIONAL WAY

Traditionally, "Mother" shed her girlfriends and flirtatious ways to take on the awesome burdens of forming her children's characters and keeping a home. "Father" lost his "wild and crazy" ways in order to provide financial security for his family.

No wonder few people remember seeing their parents in the simple acts of being playful with one another or having an intimate conversation.

SOCIETAL CHANGES

The sexual revolution and the women's movement affected many things in our society for the better, but they have not always been good for intimacy in marriage.

The sexual revolution's message that free, uncommitted, and unfettered sex was OK actually offered some destructive notions to people who were in long-standing, committed relationships and were very "fettered" by the daily realities of sharing children and living arrangements.

Some who had not experienced the "here and now" of free sex felt that they had been deprived and sought extramarital affairs. This form of "liberation" tends to undermine the stability, cooperation, and commitment necessary for developing emotional security between parents.

The women's movement also created a dilemma. There was now much more opportunity—and pressure—for women to go out into the business world and pursue careers. They were also expected to continue to raise the children, keep the home, stay physically fit, and maintain active social lives.

Men were expected to do better in their jobs, make more money, take more responsibility for the home and children, be active in community affairs, and stay in good physical shape. "Having it all" became an awful lot of work. Priorities were confused. In attempting to accomplish so much, parents had to sacrifice something. Often, it was intimacy.

PERSONAL CHANGES

Everyone, to a certain extent, has an approach/avoidance attitude toward intimacy—that very personal sharing of communication, sex, and activities. Intimacy is one of the hardest goals to achieve and one of the easiest to give up on.

Most couples circle each other like wary porcupines, fearing that they will be stabbed if they get too close. Self-exposure demands tremendous vulnerability—and trust.

In order to take this risk, an individual must develop sufficient self-esteem to cushion the shock of possible rejection.

Frequently people marry and have children before they have the opportunity to develop this self-esteem. Then, with the new physical, emotional, and financial demands of raising children, many parents throw in the towel on intimacy—often with a secret sigh of relief.

Let's look at some classic examples of what can happen when couples allow their parenting relationships to eclipse their personal needs for intimacy. These descriptions are exaggerated to make a point, and no couple or family will fit entirely into any one category. In truth, to varying degrees, some aspects of each of these situations exist in all of our lives.

Mommy and Daddy

The song title, "Two Different Worlds," best describes these parents. The division of sex roles is very rigid: He brings home the bacon and she cooks it. He is responsible for achieving financial security for the family and she is responsible for raising the children and running the household. And never the twain shall meet.

He wouldn't know what size underwear the children wear, what to ask the teacher on conference day, or how to plan nutritious meals.

She wouldn't know an IRA from a CD account, how to start the lawn mower, or where their life insurance policies are kept.

When they ask each other, "How was your day?" they don't expect much of an answer. She presumes that he is not interested in hearing the daily accounts of the children's lives, and he assumes that she is neither interested in nor capable of understanding his masculine world.

What happens to a couple who live in such separate worlds is that their personal identities disappear and they perceive themselves and each other solely in terms of parenting roles.

Eventually, they may even refer to each other as "Mommy" and "Daddy."

Beware: before you know it, "Mommy" and "Daddy" turn into "Gram" and "Gramps."

Busy Bees

These two attractive and successful people are envied by many for their ability to "have it all." Their home life resembles a well-run beehive with all family members buzzing around in constant activity and energetically pursuing work objectives.

Weeknights are busy times for all family members. The children have their homework to do and their instruments to practice on, while "Mother Bee" flies off to classes in yoga, gourmet Chinese cooking, and dog obedience training. "Father Bee's" weeknights are filled with racquetball, poker, and staying at the office to tie up loose ends. One evening a week the busy bees attend parent effectiveness training class together.

Their children participate in anything and everything the community has to offer, from orchestra conducting for preschoolers to bobsled racing for the gifted and talented. On the rare occasions when there are no planned activities the children quickly become bored and demand, "What can we do now?"

The only unscheduled time that the family has together during the entire week is from 1:00 to 4:00 P.M. on Sundays. Usually they go to a movie.

Busy bees are so busy being busy that their skills for either developing or maintaining intimacy are doomed to atrophy. Although their rapid pace creates the appearance of an active and fulfilling lifestyle, it tends to camouflage a lack of intimacy between them.

The danger in spending so little time together is the lack of opportunities to relax with each other, to air grievances, and to share what is going on in their daily lives. The busy bees need to slow down and spend some time getting to know each other at a more personal level rather than being diverted by their activities.

The Buddies

The "buddies" are an androgynous-looking couple who agree completely on one thing: children's needs always come first. The polar opposites of the "Me" generation, they are consumed with meeting their children's needs (real or imagined) to the complete extinction of any needs they might have as individuals or with one another.

For these two, sexuality and parenthood go together about as well as imported champagne and Cheerios.

Everyone's personality has three component parts: the parent, the child, and the adult. The *parent* part serves as a conscience for guiding moral choices. The *child* part functions to engage in spontaneous and pleasurable activities, and the *adult* part helps to balance the often conflicting needs of the parent and child.

With the buddies, the parent dominates and deprives this "child within" of opportunities for spontaneity and pleasure. In their full-scale devotion to being good parents, they are guilty of child neglect—with respect to the children within themselves. The buddies are lacking an essential element of intimacy in their inability to be fun-loving or feel temporarily carefree.

The Kids

The most predominant characteristics of the "kids" is their closeness with their own parents. They eat at his parents' house on Friday and at hers on Sunday. They bowl with his folks on Tuesday and play pinochle with her parents on Thursday. His and her parents enjoy dropping in on the kids whenever they're in the neighborhood.

In their own relationship the kids behave like either a parent or a child with each other. She tends to whine when she is unhappy, pout when she is angry, and become tentative when she wants to ask him for something. On the other hand, she will scold him for being too quiet at a party, gently remind him to eat a better breakfast, and tell him in no uncertain terms when he must be home at night.

He, too, feels most comfortable in relating to her as a parent or a child. He punishes her with silence for spending too much money, reprimands her for being disorganized about the house, and instructs her on the proper stroke to improve her tennis game. This stern patriarch also acts like a little boy, looking forlorn when he wants affection, asking her to pick out what he should wear, and waiting helplessly for her to boil water for his morning cup of coffee.

Attempts to communicate on an adult level have been disastrous. When he tried to convey feelings of insecurity about his work, she became frightened and could not be supportive. When she communicated some of her sexual needs to him, he heard this as criticism of his masculinity and reacted in a hurt and angry manner.

The kids were just beginning to realize that they needed to communicate more openly if their relationship was going to survive. However, just at this critical and fragile juncture, something happened that made the possibility of developing a close relationship as remote as having tea on Mars. The kids had a kid of their own.

Now this couple can comfortably use their new parent identities as glue to cover up the cracks in their personal relationships. They can deflect their prior frustrations into the socially acceptable roles of being "good parents."

These four couples illustrate some common dilemmas that parents experience in achieving intimacy. The demands of children, at any stage, will place tremendous obstacles in the way of parents trying to keep their own relationship alive. Yet the rewards of intimacy, including self-acceptance, open communication, sexual fulfillment, and mutual support, are well worth the trouble.

NURTURING INTIMACY

Parents need determination as well as new approaches for confronting the challenge of combining intimacy with parenthood. Here are some suggestions that can help establish or restore intimacy to your relationship. Now all you need is determination.

Spend Time Alone Regularly

Spending time alone when children are young is especially difficult. However, if you fail to have periodic intimate moments at this stage, the chances of becoming "Mommy and Daddy" increase dramatically every year.

Taking a walk around the block or sharing a cocktail in the living room can provide the necessary time for staying in touch with one another. Your children will soon learn that they must respect your private time together.

Hire baby-sitters even for brief periods of time. Find other parents with whom you can exchange child care. A weekend away from the children, even at an in-town hotel, may seem like the equivalent of a week in Hawaii for a couple without children.

Maintain Personal Friendships

Many of us neglect personal friendships after marriage. We feel that we have the only friend we really need—our spouse. Expecting one person to meet all of our needs is both unrealistic and unfair.

Don't feel guilty about actively maintaining other relationships. If you have a phone conversation in the evening with a friend, you are not "leaving him all alone," just as you are not "abandoning her" if you spend an evening out with friends.

Share Life Maintenance Activities

To avoid living in separate worlds and speaking different languages, parents need to take an interest in and, to some extent, participate in each other's domain.

Together, itemize all household chores, child care responsibilities, financial dealings, and miscellaneous errands that need to be handled on a regular basis. Also, make a note of who takes responsibility for each item.

Review this list from time to time to see which of these items could be shared or exchanged. For example, a husband, unfamiliar with his child's teacher, attends a semester conference. A wife, not accustomed to paying the monthly bills, assumes that responsibility. Sharing these obligations will increase the opportunity for joint decision making and mutual support.

Make Dates

Just as you would make an appointment to have your teeth cleaned, start developing the habit of setting aside time with each other for activities like going out to dinner, making love, or discussing concerns that have come up during the week.

Most people wait for this time to become available as if by magic. With children, it rarely does.

Initially, making a date to make love on Friday night may seem awkward and "unspontaneous." However, putting time aside to be together is paradoxically the best way to ensure opportunities for spontaneous interactions.

Appreciate Each Other

Many couples take one another for granted. We do a terrific job of nurturing our children's developing personalities by giving them the praise and affirmation they need, but we assume that, as adults, we should be finished growing up, and thus we neglect to give each other this essential support.

Take off your "habit glasses" and try seeing each other with new lenses. Give frequent compliments about things you would normally take for granted, such as appearance, meal preparations, job performance, home repairs, and dealings with children. Be as specific as possible. Instead of saying, "You look good," say, "I really like the way the color of your shirt brings out the blue in your eyes."

Balance the Children's Needs with Your Own

Weekend activities and vacations are frequently planned with the sole focus on what would be good for the children. Begin to approach weekend and travel planning with a recognition that both your needs and your children's deserve consideration.

Finally, it is important to remember that you are your children's most significant role models. If you make room for intimacy in your marriage, chances are good that your children will do the same when they become parents.

Take Charge of the Power Hour: Making Evening Hours Count

Jim Anderson smiles as he opens the front door to his home. Although it's late afternoon, his step is light, and his three-piece suit looks freshly pressed. He calls out, "Margaret, I'm home!"

Margaret, his fashionably dressed wife, greets him with kisses and cheerful words of welcome. In the background the three Anderson children calmly descend the stairway to complete the happy scene.

The opening segment of the popular television sitcom "Father Knows Best" is Hollywood's version of how it's "supposed to be" at day's end. If this type of calm, happy scene is replayed in your home on a daily basis, this chapter isn't for you.

If, on the other hand, events at your house are chaotic, explosive, harried, noisy, or confusing at day's end, you are experiencing the "power hour" in a more typical way.

The power hour is that time in late afternoon or early evening when family members reunite. Each one is anxious to share the day's events—rewards, hassles, worries, silly incidents. We shed our daytime roles, kick off our shoes, and plant ourselves in a favorite easy chair. The comfortable sensations of home and family overtake us.

But unless your family operates as smoothly as the Andersons—and I don't know of many that do—this is a critical time period. Each family member brings home a different level of physical and emotional energy and individual expectations and needs. When everyone begins competing for attention, mass confusion can result.

The intensity of the power hour can spread positive and happy feelings. If you've had a great day and come home whistling, your infectious good humor can rub off on everyone else in the family.

But the intensity can also be negative: feelings are on the surface and can easily be hurt.

WHEN IS THE "POWER HOUR"?

The power hour varies from household to household and can shift from day to day. In the family where the woman is homemaker and cares for the children during the day the power hour begins the minute Dad comes through the door.

When both parents work outside the home the power hour starts rolling as soon as the children are collected from day care or school.

In single-parent households, the power hour stretches until the children are tucked in for the night.

Interestingly enough, the negative kind of power hour is widely recognized by law enforcement agencies, though they don't use the same name. They report that many calls about family squabbles, child abuse, and requests for restraining orders trace back to problems that originated in the early evening hours. The crux of the problem, one officer told me, is that no one is listening to anyone else. Sound familiar?

So how can you make sure the power hour at your house is as calm and pleasant as possible?

EXPECTATIONS, NEEDS, AND SCHEDULES

The first step is to sit down with your mate and discuss your expectations. Expectations, whether stated out loud or established in routine behavior, stem from those well-ingrained messages you received as children. They are adopted as part of your attitude. Sit back and examine the source of your attitudes.

Ask yourself and your spouse about the events occurring during the power hour when you were a child. When your father came home, did your mother hold you and your problems back until he had a chance to unwind? Traditionally this has been the case, so husbands and fathers may have an unspoken expectation: husbands come home, the kids are under control, and dinner is ready. But how does the rest of the family feel?

If you had your wish, what would happen when you first met with the whole family? What do your mate and children expect? How similar are your expectations?

Next, think about your needs and your family's needs. In general, how do you feel at this time of day? Do you need time to switch from your daytime role to that of family member? Do you need quiet? Do you need care and soothing?

Parents who stay at home during the day may need adult conversation and stimulation with someone more communicative than a two-year-old. When both parents work they may feel they need to give "quality" time to their child.

Take a hard look at your family structure, too. When do mates return home? How frequently do unpredictable events interfere? Are both parents on the same time schedule? What about the children's schedules?

When you've identified your expectations and those of your spouse, when you've listed your needs and the needs of your family, and when you've outlined typical schedules, you're ready to take charge.

TAKING CHARGE

The simple part about taking charge is that you already have all the tools. The best part of the options are all yours. The passwords are *trade-offs* and *flexibility*—or good old-fashioned teamwork.

Trade-offs use your natural ability to give and take. If dinner must be cooked and bath time and bedtime rituals observed, trade off! If one mate is especially tired or hassled, the other can assume the responsibilities and give the other a rest period. (The obvious key to making this method work is flexibility.) For a day or two you may feel you're getting the short end of the stick, but things usually have a way of balancing out.

Your plans should contain a degree of "wiggle room" so that you can cope with unforeseen events. Very often interruptions affect your daily routines. A young child who suddenly develops a high fever and expresses a justifiably cranky attitude can quickly interfere with an otherwise peaceful evening. Likewise, a hard day at home or in the office can produce a short-tempered spouse who is less apt to cope successfully with the power hour. While you cannot predict or prevent those events, you can learn to adjust to them as long as your personalized scheme allows for it.

A good example of trade-offs and flexibility can be found in one family where Mom is home with a sixteen-month-old baby and Dad does the mealtime cleanup. "During the power hour," Mom says, "I give him part of the action." They switch their afternoon routines back and forth. Dad takes over the care of their son while she cooks. Mom begins bedtime preparations while Dad does the mealtime clean-up.

Couples who work outside the home typically contend with more chaos during the power hour. In another family both husband and wife are teachers and were quick to identify with afternoon confusion. Their children are ages two, four, and seven. While they switch and trade off, and use a good deal of flexibility in doing so, they've added another dimension to their solution. They call it *passing*.

When it seems that emotions are running high and chaos looms in the background, each family member has the right to say, "I think I'll pass on that." In other words, "Let's deal with that later." This family recognizes the importance of shelving emotionally charged issues until a time when they can be more easily handled. Minimizing hot issues has helped them solve difficulties that needn't be resolved in an atmosphere of pandemonium.

A husband and wife team of marriage and family counselors have minimized their power hour battles with a daily "tea party." Since each partner arrives home at a different time, the parent who is first to return greets their boys, ages three and four, and enlists their help in "tea time" preparations.

When the other parent returns the four sit at the kitchen table and enjoy an afternoon snack and a cup of tea. The gathering fulfills several needs. One is that the boys have a chance for undivided attention and can comfortably reestablish closeness with working parents. The other is that the parents have a built-in checking-in period, when they test the emotional waters, stress levels, fatigue, and general coping ability of each other and the children.

The father says, "These tea parties give us a happy situation that reduces competition." He grinned as he added that children typically can't sit for long periods of time "talking" with adults, so after fifteen or twenty minutes they are happy to return to play activities.

Following are nine steps that you and your family can take to make your power hour as peaceful as possible.

NINE STEPS TO CONQUERING THE POWER HOUR

1. Make a schedule that shows when everyone arrives home. Take into account days when late meetings, health club visits, doctor's appointments, and such demand that you be especially flexible.

2. Keep a running list of chores that must be accomplished and negotiate a trade-off system with your mate. Dinner, light housework, bath time, and evening dishes may be a few of the chores that will appear on your list.

3. Check in with your family as a whole before members begin to scatter. Help reduce competition by briefly sharing the day's events and listen while others do the same thing. This period gives everyone a chance to test the waters and determine stress levels, fatigue, and general coping ability.

4. Examine your expectations as well as those of your spouse. Are they realistic? How similar are they? Consider what other family members expect; then meet on neutral ground. Remember, your moods and behavior when you return home affect the entire family.

5. Be flexible. If a neighbor or friend drops in for a surprise visit at this time of day, or if one of you is particularly tired, roll with the punches and make spontaneous changes. Trade routines. You can even the score later.

6. Make a pact to keep power hour conversations low-key and free of hot issues. If a sore point comes up, agree to table the discussion until you're more relaxed and the children are tucked in for the night. This will help smooth out the problem in a calmer atmosphere.

7. Sensitize yourself to seasonal moods and changes. During the summer months, for example, moods are likely to be more carefree, and routine chores will be pushed later into the evening as families spend more time outdoors. On the other hand, the winter months may cause unpredictable

hardships. A broken furnace or hazardous driving conditions can try anyone's patience.

8. Review your plan every few months. Look at your schedule and see if any major changes have occurred that affect the family. Moving, a new baby, and changed work schedules can all turn your plan topsy-turvy. Revise your plan, if necessary.

9. Above all, don't panic if you lose control. Nobody's perfect!

Grandparents

What is a grandparent?

The popular, perennial image is sugar and spice and everything nice. Storybook grandparents love to baby-sit. They always have time to bake cookies and play games. And they never, never interfere, argue, or criticize their grandchildren's parents.

Yet one mother has this to say:

"My mother lives close enough to come by every week. When she does she stays until the baby goes to bed. Then she starts on me. Am I feeding him right, clothing him adequately, disciplining him enough? She often asks him 'if mama is treating you right.' It got so bad that my husband finally told her she was being too possessive with the baby and it was interfering with our attitudes toward her and thereby influencing the baby's emotions toward her."

Grandparents—whether they be your spouse's parents or your own—can be an invaluable resource or an intolerable irritant. They can happily baby-sit at a moment's notice or never make an effort to see their grandchild. They can creatively share skills, experience, and know-how, or they can berate and belittle you until your tolerance and your confidence as a parent are destroyed.

This chapter will discuss the spectrum from "positive" to "problem" grandparents and how you can learn to live happily with the family you have.

POSITIVE GRANDPARENTING

Positive grandparenting is a pleasure for all concerned. Grandparents get to enjoy the child without the responsibility of being a parent. Parents get the benefit of loving care for the child. And the child gets his own personal care giver, storyteller, historian, mentor, wizard, confidant, negotiator, counselor, and role model.

Positive grandparents are the kind of grandparents every child deserves. They give pleasure all through the childhood years, guidance through the teenage years, comforting memories through the adult years. They are a person's link to history and probably the best source of unconditional love around. If your in-laws and parents are positive grandparents to your children, count your blessings. It isn't always so.

POSITIVE BUT ABSENT GRANDPARENTS

Some grandparents would like to be positive, but for a variety of reasons cannot be. Often they live too far away for frequent and regular visits. If this is the case, when your child is old enough you can fill the gap somewhat by keeping in touch through cassette tapes, telephone calls, letters, and pictures. Talk with your child often about Grandma and Grandpa. Make word pictures and reinforce them with photographs. Then, when the child and the grandparents do visit, there will be some degree of familiarity.

Other grandparents might be burdened with financial problems—maybe they can't afford to buy nice things for their grandchildren or take them places. You should know if this is

the case with your parents or in-laws and be able to help with the assurance that love doesn't cost anything to get or to give.

Your parents or in-laws may also be consciously trying not to interfere with your child rearing and your family structure. They may have taken to heart some hint or outspoken request of yours that they visit only when they're invited. Many parents hold back because they want to let you live your own life and are reluctant to be there with advice, assistance, or suggestions before they are asked for.

NEGATIVE GRANDPARENTS

Another kind of grandparent is the one who doesn't seem to want to have anything to do with your child.

For some people the very idea of being a grandparent is depressing. It is not a state a person chooses, and no matter how young the person is, having a grandchild indicates age. In today's youth-oriented society, being a grandparent is a sign of maturity and as such is strongly resented by some. If this is the case with your parents or in-laws, all you can do is hope that they will change their minds.

Sometimes the standoffish grandparent is staying away not because of lack of love or concern but because of a real reluctance to take on added responsibilities or get involved in more child rearing. Many people with grown children feel they have already paid their dues. Now that their kids are gone they are ready to go out and start on some perhaps long-delayed dreams—trips, new jobs, new activities, old activities picked up again, new and old friends, each other.

Into this idyll of peacefulness comes a son or daughter with a brand-new family, requesting baby-sitting service, live-in help, or financial assistance. One grandmother put it this way:

"Our children are grown with children of their own. My husband and I have started planning the second stage of our lives together. We are still young: we can go back to school or travel or start up a new business. There are all sorts of possibilities—and one problem.

"My children have children—and they have decided I'm a full-time baby-sitter. I'm willing to share my experience, my know-how, and my skills. But to go back to having infants and toddlers around all the time, with dirty diapers, strewn toys, and exhaustion—that isn't my ideal lifestyle now."

If your parents or in-laws live nearby but don't often visit, take a close look at the expectations you have of them.

Do you call them up at dinner time and want to take the children an hour later for the whole evening? Do you get angry or offended when they refuse such a request? Do you bristle when an observation is offered, yet expect a sympathetic, listening ear when your responsibilities leave you feeling overextended?

Positive grandparenting is a labor of love, not something that can be forced. A word of appreciation and gratitude can go a long way, too. For a parent to hear an adult child say, "Now I know how much work babies are; I appreciate all the more what you've done for me," can smooth a rocky relationship considerably.

PROBLEM GRANDPARENTS

There's yet another kind of grandparent: the one who is so concerned and so excited that he or she tries to take over. This grandparent give suggestions, advice, and lectures at every turn. Knowingly or unknowingly, he or she is undermining your confidence and authority to a point at which the relationship is endangered. These "problem" parents and parents-in-law are often seen as competing with new parents for the love and control of babies and small children.

How do you handle the situation when you feel that your parent or parent-in-law—or anyone, for that matter—is overstepping bounds, infringing on your rights as a parent, or undermining your confidence in your ability to do what is best for your son or daugher?

Begin by realizing that there will always be differences of opinion. But you don't have to raise your child as your parents raised you or as your parents-in-law raised your spouse. Your child is your responsibility, and you have the final say.

But that doesn't mean you can't listen.

You can listen and shrug. You can listen and argue. You can listen and laugh. You can listen and take the advice. You will probably do all of these things at different times.

A good tactic is to try to see the problem from another point of view. You may never be able to take your mother's advice graciously about bathing the baby, but if you can get along with her in other areas, then make those your main focus and let the bathing dispute slide. Most often a possessive grandparent sincerely wants to help. We all express ourselves in a different way. You don't have to change people to get along with them; you just take the best and let the rest go.

Both parents and grown children will also do well to remember that the two most harmful words in the English language are *should* and *ought*. *Need, must,* and *have to* are not far behind. And all these words are especially hurtful when preceded by the pronoun *you.*

"You should listen to me!"

"You ought to want to baby-sit so I can go back to work!"

MAKING THE BEST OF IT

In listening to parents who have come through stressful periods with interfering grandparents there are three ideas that come across again and again:

1. *If you have a problem, talk to the person directly about it.* One of the benefits of being a grown-up is that you are entitled to your own opinion. If you are having problems with parental interference, make them known. Have an honest and direct talk with the person who is troubling you.

    Tell the person who is interfering that you know he or she loves your baby but that you are responsible for the child and you insist that certain procedures be followed. Then list them.

    You are responsible for rules of health, safety, conduct, and discipline. No doubt both the grandparents and the child will feel happier not having to invent rules. The child will definitely do better with consistent discipline. Make clear that you are acting in your child's best interest, and you will most likely get cooperation. At any rate, you will feel better for having made your feelings known.

    It might also be that a child is creating problems between his parents and grandparents by playing them against one another. He's testing limits—"At home I get to stay up till 11:00," or "At Grandma's I get all the cookies I want." A calm discussion between adults will usually uncover the problem, and establishing strict limits will bring the situation under control.

2. *Be thankful that your children have grandparents who love them.* Think about what your grandparents meant to

you. Then think about what your children's grandparents are capable of giving them. It is far, far better for a child to have too much love than too little.

3. *No one can replace Mom and Dad.* Think about the way you love your children. It's a very special love. By the same token, the love your children have for you is very special. No matter how much you think a parent or an in-law is trying to win your baby's affection away from you, no matter how much you fear that your child will turn to the other for love and comfort, you don't really have to worry. Your child knows who her mother and father are. There isn't any real competition in her mind—you are special and no one else can ever take your place, no matter how hard he or she tries.

For children, no matter how old they are, relationships with parents can be mine fields of doubt, fear, anger, blame, guilt, and resentment. Slights and recriminations from childhood hurt as much now as they did then. Parents' refusal to see grown children as they really are results in hard feelings, harsh words, and unfulfilled expectations.

But parents are not infallible. They are not giants. They are just people trying, however poorly, to do their best. Being able to accept them with all their weaknesses and foibles is another step in the growing-up process. It's what you hope your children will do for you when the time comes. With love and luck, the result will be that parents accept children and children accept parents as unique, worthwhile individuals—warts and all.

Teaching Children Traffic Safety

The statistics are grim.

Each year thousands of children are killed in pedestrian accidents. Most of the accidents occur between 3:00 and 6:00 in the afternoon within two blocks of a child's home, on straight stretches of road where the cars are going less than 30 miles per hour.

The most common type of accident involving young children is called *dart-out* or *mid-block dash*. This happens when a child suddenly runs out into the roadway without looking. Backing-up accidents and accidents involving children who are walking or playing in a driveway or roadway are also common.

These tragedies happen so frequently because young children simply have no conception of the danger of moving vehicles. Their idea of traffic is often limited to the family car, the ambulance, and the fire engine. They are completely unaware of traffic laws—red lights, green lights, yield signs, blind curves. They don't know instinctively that cars can hurt them.

Preschoolers have short attention spans. They are impulsive

and inherently curious. They think of only one thing at a time, and if a parent, a friend, or an ice cream truck is on the other side of the street, they will go there without hesitation or caution.

Physically, preschoolers are at a disadvantage. The height of three- to five-year-olds makes them see vehicles much differently than adults do. Stoop, sit, or kneel at a roadside to get a feel for this difference. You can't see nearly as much, and the perspective is very confusing, making it difficult to tell whether a vehicle is coming, going, or standing still.

A preschooler's vision, hearing, and reaction time are also undeveloped. All these factors together mean that toddlers and very young children simply are not developmentally capable of understanding and coping with traffic. But it is possible to begin teaching them the basics of traffic safety after taking into account all the characteristics that make them vulnerable.

Unsupervised children run the greatest risk of being accident victims, of course. Your child will obviously be safest when you're watching her and holding her hand as she crosses a street.

But the fact is that you will not always be there, and even if you could be, it takes only a second for a toddler who's gotten away from you to dash out from between parked cars into the path of an oncoming vehicle.

You won't always be able to hold her hand, either, as she gets older, broadens her horizons, and goes to school. You need to help her lay a good foundation of safety habits now so that you and she can build on it as she grows. You can add more freedom and responsibility as she demonstrates the ability to handle it.

What can you do to train your preschooler to respect streets and traffic and to ensure that she will remember the lessons when you're not present?

You can, of course, try to isolate her from traffic altogether, which is probably impossible. Alternately, you can start a gradual training program.

From the time a child starts walking to about age two she can be learning the names of things in the traffic environment: *street, yard, road, car.* From two to three she can be taught where to play, to walk, to stop. At four she can understand the dangers posed by moving, parked, and backing-up vehicles and how to look for cars in the street.

After age four you can add more abstract concepts of directions and what signs mean. By five a child is capable of learning to cross a street safely at mid-block, and by six she should be able to obey traffic light signals at intersections by herself.

WHERE TO PLAY

The first thing a toddler must learn is that there is a difference between places where people walk and play and places where trucks, buses, and cars park and drive. Show your child this by getting down on your hands and knees and pointing out exactly where the grass or curb ends and where the pavement or street begins. Talk about the difference between streets and sidewalks, driveways and yards, playgrounds and parking lots.

Set Boundaries

When your child goes outside alone, give him a boundary. Select boundaries based on the child's maturity, the location of your home, the amount of traffic, and the amount of supervision. Make the boundary absolute: *this is as far as you can go and no farther.*

Perhaps the boundary you set will be the sidewalk in front of your house and the bushes on either side. Or it can be the corner of an apartment building or the edge of a driveway—any demarcation that you can put your finger on and that doesn't move.

A note here: if you make your child's approved play area as interesting as possible, you will have much less trouble getting him to stay inside the boundaries. A sandbox, something to climb, crawl into, or swing on will keep a child happily occupied for hours. A bare yard or a play area will soon have him looking around for something more interesting to do.

As part of boundary setting you also need to designate areas for riding wheeled toys. It's a lot more fun to ride on pavement than on grass, and you can be sure your child will find that out posthaste. Whether the sidewalk, driveway, or pavement at your home is safe is an individual situation, but your child must know that he can never ride his wheeled toy into the street under any circumstances.

After you've set the boundaries, it is up to you to enforce them. The hardest part is making sure you are absolutely consistent. It may be necessary for you to drop everything else for the time this training takes: you'll have to watch your toddler every minute and bring him inside or take other appropriate action each and every time he steps outside the boundary.

WHERE TO WALK AND STOP

Your child will not learn about traffic safety through punishments, scoldings, warnings, or memorization of lists of safety rules. These negative approaches tell the child what *not* to do, when he actually needs to know exactly what it is he *should* do.

What he should do, of course, is walk on the sidewalk or grass and *stop* every time he comes to a street. Teach him this by direct experience. Take him for walks. Hold his hand and walk between him and the street. Stop at every driveway or street, giving him cues for doing so (a voice command or a squeeze of the hand). If a child believes he absolutely must stop at every street, he will be much less likely to run out blindly when you are not there to restrain him.

BY EXAMPLE WE TEACH

Example is the key to the success you'll have in teaching your preschooler traffic safety. A child learns by imitating those around her—mainly her parents. This means that *you* must stop at every street, even if you can see at a glance that there is no traffic. If you dash across the street against the light, if you don't stop, look, and listen at every corner, then you cannot be surprised or upset when your child does the same.

CROSSING STRAIGHT STRETCHES

After a child knows she must stop at streets, you can teach her the more advanced concepts of looking both ways for approaching vehicles and determining the vehicle's direction of travel.

Get down on the child's level. Point first to the left and then to the right, saying each time, "This is the way we look for cars coming." Have the child point in one direction, look, and say whether there are any cars, trucks, buses, motorcycles, or bicycles coming. Turn the other way and repeat the same actions: point, look, confirm. (It's better not to use the words *left* and *right*. *One way* and *the other way* are adequate.)

Point out that a car coming gets bigger as it comes. A car going away gets smaller. Ask the child to listen for cars, too; you can often hear a vehicle before you can see it.

When your child has practiced this for a while, let her lead you across the streets. Gentle reminders are sometimes necessary. Practice until the actions are fairly consistent.

MISTAKES AND PROBLEMS

Children will forget to stop. They'll forget to look and listen. A mistake is part of learning, and the best advantage can be made of it by talking about it, encouraging thinking and problem solving. After all, traffic situations change constantly, so there is never one right answer for every situation. Discussing mistakes calmly makes them part of the learning process.

In addition, mistakes are often made because children can't see adequately. They can't see, for instance, over or around parked cars or fences. Snowdrifts or bushes sometimes obstruct vision. During the learning process, select places for crossing where the view from the *child's* height is unobstructed.

BACKING UP AND DRIVEWAYS

Learning to distinguish whether a car is coming toward you or going away from you is a skill that takes practice. Learning to recognize a vehicle that is backing up is another important skill.

Many accidents happen in driveways, because the operator cannot see a child in back of the vehicle while backing. Teach your child about backing up by listening to the sound of a car starting in a driveway. Show him the smoke from the exhaust. Point out the backup lights. Instruct him to get out of the way quickly when he sees a vehicle start to back up.

It also helps to explain to a child that the reason we stop at streets and get out of the way of backing-up cars is because they will hurt us if they hit us. It's easier for children to remember to stay out of the street if they understand why they cannot be there when a car is coming.

CROSSING AT INTERSECTIONS

So far we've talked about crossing straight, uncomplicated streets at mid-block. By the time a child is four or five she will be moving farther and farther from home, and it's time to learn about crossing at intersections.

Intersections are confusing from a child's point of view. You have to look for traffic from at least three directions and decide whether a vehicle from any of those directions will turn onto the street you're crossing. You also have to realize that vehicles and pedestrians travel at different rates of speed, and you have to compensate for that.

Take your child to an intersection and observe the traffic flow. Ask questions: Why do some cars stop and others don't? What does it mean when a car's turn signal is on? Explain about crosswalks but explain that, even though drivers are supposed to yield right-of-way to pedestrians in crosswalks, they don't always do so, and therefore the child must learn to walk defensively.

Talk about the shapes, colors, and meanings of stop and yield signs and what drivers and pedestrians do when they see each type of sign.

INTERSECTIONS WITH LIGHTS

Go to different corners and look at traffic signals. Explain that the signal you pay attention to is the one directly across the street from you, that you can go when it is green, but that you still have to look and make sure all the cars have stopped.

When the light is above the intersection rather than on a corner post, it will be more difficult for the child to see. Tell her to watch the light as she approaches the corner. Always emphasize that, even if a walker has a green light, she must stop and look to make sure that all the cars have stopped and that none is turning onto the street she's crossing.

It may help your child to understand intersections if you can take him to a high place (the second or third floor of a building, for instance) and look down on the traffic pattern. Talk about what the cars are doing and why.

Make sure your child knows that red is for stop, yellow for wait, and green for go. Reassure him that the light will turn green if he waits but that he should always wait on the sidewalk back from the curb.

Letting a child go—to a friend's, to the store, to school—by herself is a fearful event for a parent, no doubt about it. But if you've taken the time to instruct your youngster carefully and fully, you have done as much as you can toward assuring her safety.

SET AN EXAMPLE

Have you ever crossed the street against traffic?

Sure, we've all done it. And I thought about it recently while standing on a cold, windy street corner. Then up walked a young father and a small boy of two or three who had a firm grasp on his father's hand. He stared at me curiously, as young children do, while we waited for the light to change.

I was ready to dash across the street but was very conscious of this father and son. What kind of example would I set for this young fellow? It seemed to me more important to stand there under that brown-eyed gaze and freeze if I had to than to provoke the question: "Why did that lady run across the street?"

We set examples for other people's children, too.

MORE INFORMATION

The American Automobile Association produces a set of five booklets about traffic safety for parents and children from 2½ to six years old. The set includes a *Parents' Guide for Action* and four age-graded story booklets to reinforce the concepts discussed in this chapter.

Contact your local association office for more information.

Parental Decisions: Setting Reasonable Limits for Children

Should we give permission or not?

That's the question that bedevils temporarily insecure parents confronted with "I wanna watch the monster show," or "I want sump'n else to eat," or (at ten minutes to lunchtime) "Goin' to Brad's, Mom. See ya later."

Mothers and fathers alike recognize the pattern. From dawn until dark it can be a series of—

"Let me do this!"

"Can I do that?"

"When are we goin' to the park?"

It's not enough for you to decide on the right food to eat, clothes to wear, shots to get. With their never-ending deluge of questions, youngsters can make parenting seem like an overtime session at the Supreme Court.

Few people really enjoy making tough choices, especially when a decision means that one or more persons might end up disappointed or even angry.

How easy or difficult the final decision is often depends on how familiar you are with the details of a particular request. For example, if Betsy asks again to do the same thing she sought permission for yesterday, her parents' reaction will probably be based on how yesterday's venture worked out. Good experiences usually receive endorsement the second time around. Near disasters, however, are almost sure to be shelved until future notice; for example, "No more swimming in the river or rock quarry until I say so."

So there you are, a conscientious and concerned parent who wants to do the very best for your child. But you also worry about how to explain why when you say "no."

There must be an easier way to make those decisions, you say, and you're right. This article outlines the details of a simple, four-part method you can refer to when confronted with an unfamiliar request from your child. Not only will this approach make your judgment calls less burdensome; it will also give you a chance to clarify the behavior you expect from your offspring.

Think of a pie cut into four equal pieces. The pieces represent behavioral limits as seen in the accompanying diagram.

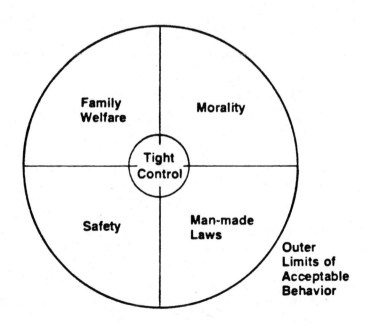

- *Morality.* This area represents the limits set by your personal moral standards.
- *Man-made laws.* This area describes the limits of acceptable behavior as set by law enforcement agencies.
- *Safety.* This area includes any activity potentially dangerous to mental or physical health.
- *Family welfare.* This area covers behavior as it relates to the shifting needs and preferences of your family group.

In the very center of the pie is an area the size of a silver dollar that represents the very tight control under which unsure and hesitant parents raise their children. The outer rim of the pie represents reasonable limits.

THE CENTER

Let's start with the silver-dollar-sized area in the center of the pie. Parents who believe that a short rein now produces desirable behavior later on keep their children inside this limit. Some parents succeed with this method. Unfortunately, however, this tight parenting style can produce rebellious youngsters who resent the smothering. And the revolters are likely to try to break out of these unreasonable set boundaries in a rush.

The results are seldom attractive. A break of this type, beginning in the child's adolescence, can lead to an emotional split that both parents and grown children regret in later years. Few scenes are sadder than those of parents and adult children estranged over a sea of silence, especially when the initial rift may have been the result of insufficient freedom granted during the formative years.

Back to the example of the pie. For purposes of this exercise, think of the outer rim of the pie as the limits of acceptable behavior for your child. Actions that fall between the silver dollar and the outer rim are all OK. But what limits do the wedges represent?

FIRST LIMIT—MORALITY

Let the first wedge of the pie represent the law of God,

morality, ethics, whatever standard you use to determine right from wrong. It will be helpful to note here that some new parents, dissatisfied with the too-tight or too-loose limits of right and wrong learned in their own childhoods, have not yet taken time to formulate a clear-cut statement of what they themselves believe to be the correct limits for acceptable behavior. If that is even partially the case with you, this exercise may help you clarify your own value system.

For example, little Socko tugs on his jeans and pleads, "Can I take my bike to school today? Everybody's ridin' in," or "I wanna play in the street." What say ye, parent? Will it be yes or no? Suggestion: check your reaction in the moral quadrant first. In your opinion, is it sinful or immoral for Socko to play in the street or use his bike under these circumstances? Probably not. That means his request has cleared the first of four measures of reasonable limits.

SECOND LIMIT—LEGALITY

Now consider the limits set by man-made laws, which make up the second wedge of the pie. Anyone moving beyond the limits set down by the FBI or by state, county, or local police flirts with arrest and/or possible punishment. The second quadrant, the law of humans, decides whether or not an action is legal.

The second of your four criteria is: Is Socko's request illegal? Can you, he, or both be put into jail for letting him take his bike to school? Hardly. Now you are already halfway to a prudent choice. Two more wedges of the pie in terms of your own standards and you will have some assurance about whether to grant permission.

THIRD LIMIT—SAFETY

The going gets trickier here in the third wedge, the province of the law of safety. You realize that very safe behavior would be under that part of the silver dollar in the pie's center. Actually, the least hazardous place for Socko would be in bed 24 hours a

day. But few parents keep such tight reins on their children, even though some might like to do so during moments of maximum frustration.

Degrees of safety are difficult to determine. Sometimes the proper response might be "It depends." For example, playing in the street can be safe or risky, depending on the street, the normal traffic flow, and the time of day. Playing in a quiet dead-end street at 11:00 A.M. with mom nearby, Socko runs few risks. However, he'd be much more vulnerable to serious harm if given the same freedom on Main Street during rush hour.

As another example, few adults would knowingly set a seven-year-old loose in an automobile with the engine running. To do so would be both irresponsible and foolish. Such behavior would be well outside the limits of the safety quadrant.

But there will be exceptions. Some farm children, for example, will have been checked out on the family tractor by age seven. With proper instruction, clearly stated limits, and a few practice runs, a cooperative child can be a help in pulling the hay rake back to the barn when the parents are busy with other chores. In that setting, assuming adequate instruction and supervision, the seven-year-old may be the right person for the job.

So, too, with sharp instruments. Few parents encourage their children to play with potentially dangerous weapons, but the element of risk is always a factor when parents try to formulate new growth opportunities for their sons and daughters. Yet some preschoolers have proven that they can use sharp tools and utensils responsibly and safely after careful instruction. One late-working father used this tactic with his up-at-the-crack-of-dawn four-year-old: "When you want to cut the orange in half, hold your fingers here on top like this. Make sure the sharp edge is under your hand and pointed down and away from your fingers. Let's see you try it." No serious cuts ever reported.

The secret, of course, is to match the level of danger and difficulty with the child's current level of competence. The ever-present risk is that you may end up feeling mighty guilty if a trail of blood marks the route of your wailing experimenter.

If you find yourself thinking, "I'd never let *my* preschooler use a sharp knife," your strong reaction means that you have made a decision about proper limits for your child. In addition, you know the basis for that judgment—the safety factor.

A typical pattern for rookie parents is to herd their child too close to the center of the pie, rather than relaxing the apron strings so the fast-growing boy or girl can experience life challenges more in keeping with his or her present level of capability. Simply stated, most normal and healthy children are ready for more complex tasks long before receiving the parental go-ahead to prove it. The parents' goal should be to offer children as much freedom as they can handle as soon as possible, within the parent-determined boundaries of reasonable limits.

FOURTH LIMIT—FAMILY WELFARE

The final quadrant of the pie is the limit of family welfare, a much easier ground for determining whether to grant approval. An example:

In one home it's a pleasant and unhurried Sunday afternoon. Both parents are enjoying the freedom from a regular, hectic schedule to putter around or relax in front of a televised ball game. Although never stated, everyone senses that nothing major is planned until the evening meal.

Without notice, daughter Polly suddenly breezes in and announces, "I'll be at Pam's—we've got a big project going. Be home for dinner." The parents, only half listening, have already run Polly's announcement/request through each of the four limit quadrants. Pam is a good and proven friend (morality). Her mother is a fine person (morality). Pam's home is a moral, legal, and safe harbor for Polly (man-made laws). No traffic risks exist from here to there (safety). Polly's temporary absence won't upset any preset family plans (family welfare). For all these reasons the approving grunt from the vicinity of the television set effectively communicates, "Gotcha. Permission granted. See you later."

An identical scene in the same home two weeks later ends differently. When Polly announces her plans with Pam the parental reaction is "No way. We're headed for Nana's today, and we need you clean and neat for departure in exactly twenty-two minutes. Hop to it, Pol."

Today's family schedule includes a stop at Polly's grand-mother's house. For that reason what was acceptable two weeks ago is "no go" today. And even though today's requested visit to Pam's would be just as moral, legal, and safe as the last time, it doesn't match the family's plan for this Sunday afternoon.

So now, parents, you're on your own. Using this simple four-step guide in making parental decisions, you will be better prepared when you hear, "Can I do this for that reason?" Run the query through the limits represented by the four pie quarters. If the request passes muster with all four, endorse it with enthusiasm. "You bet you may. Have a good time and tell Pam's mother I said thanks for those delicious pickles." If it doesn't, explain why: "Sorry, sweetie. We're going to make a stop at Nana's today. She'd be so disappointed if you weren't along."

In each case you can feel comfortable with your decision, because the reason given makes sense in terms of your personal preferences in four key areas that affect the health and develop-ment of your growing child.

How to Survive a Fire: What to Do if Fire Strikes Your Home

Two fire stories recently were featured in the news. One reported a schoolhouse fire, where 2,000 pupils were safely evacuated in less than three minutes. The other concerned a private home, where only two out of a family of five were able to escape.

It seems odd that 2,000 people could escape from one structure but three of five should perish in another. One significant reason is that the 2,000 schoolchildren had taken part in fire drills. The family of five had not. Panic—and tragedy—resulted.

In the United States fire strikes every 45 seconds, hitting 700,000 residences a year. Three-quarters of the 6,500 fire deaths yearly occur in homes. Most result from ignorance.

PLAN AND PRACTICE FIRE DRILLS

Fire drills can avert many tragedies. Sixty-five percent of fire victims are trapped on the top floor of their homes. Half of the victims are children under age ten. A healthy adult stands a good chance of escaping, but a fire drill might mean the difference between life and death for youngsters and the elderly.

Every family ought, therefore, to work out and practice the steps to be followed in case of fire. The construction of your house, the layout of rooms, and the composition of your family will all influence the precise method of evacuating your family from the house in case of fire.

To decide on the best way, first draw up a floor plan of your house, indicating all doors and windows as well as stairways, porches, and porch or garage roofs. Indicate all escape routes from each room on your floor plan. If possible, map out at least two escape routes for every bedroom.

Statistics show that many fire victims wake up in time to escape but don't survive because they made no plans for coping with a fire emergency. They lack even a basic knowledge of fire, its behavior, its actual dangers—they may fear flames but show little respect for deadly gases, combustion, or superheated air, which kills more than 90 percent of fire victims.

Fire travels by following a rising or moving current of air. The heated air and toxic gases from a fire below rise just as smoke goes up your chimney. That air and gas can get as hot as 1,000° F. A few breaths of it can be fatal, and it can ignite draperies, furniture, or any other combustible material. By such means, a fire can spread through four or five floors in a quarter of an hour.

The basic aim of your precautions, then, should be to prevent the staircases and hallways from becoming funnels for the flames and to provide alternate means of escape, just in case.

PLANNING FOR FIRE EMERGENCIES

A few basic principles will help in working out the best emergency procedure:

- Start at the basement, where faulty heating plants start many a fire. Install a heavy door leading to the basement and close it tightly every night.
- Make sure that the windows you choose for escape can be

opened easily, even by a child or an elderly person. If screens or storm windows prevent a quick exit, consider doing without them on the escape window or replace them with some other type of window.

- Put a police whistle into each bedroom so it can be blasted to warn others. It can also be used to alert neighbors from a window. Neighbors with ladders have saved many fire victims.
- Close all bedroom doors before going to bed. A Cleveland family learned this firsthand when fire struck their home. Three children slept on the third floor. Two of them were asphyxiated by gases flowing through their open bedroom door. The third child survived because his bedroom door was closed.
- If you should wake up in the middle of the night and discover a fire, don't stand up and stumble around. Standing up will thrust your head into the midst of the deadly fire gases, which are lighter than air and collect near the ceiling. Instead, roll off the bed and crawl to the window. By staying close to the floor, you'll get more oxygen.
- Feel your bedroom door before you open it. If you can feel no heat on the door panel, open it with care. Place your weight against the door and, with your face turned away, open the door no more than an inch and feel the air that rushes through the crack. If the air is hot or there is any pressure against the door, slam it shut and turn to the alternate escape routes worked out for you and your family. Tests have shown that survival time is as short as two minutes if the door is open, compared to as many as five to eleven minutes with the door closed.
- After you open a cold door you may find that the fire has not reached the stairway and that you can escape that way. If you do, alert other family members by shouting and pounding on their doors.

In a fire that has gotten out of hand, however, your escape must be made from an upstairs bedroom. In order to get everyone out of the house safely and quickly, you need an escape plan. This escape plan is vital, because everyone must know what to do and what not to do; it can save the lives of your loved ones.

In your home fire drill planning you must figure out some way to get out of the house from the bedrooms without using the main stairs. Remember, it is up that stairway that deadly heat and poisonous gases flood a house after a fire gets started.

CAREFUL PLANNING FOR CHILDREN'S SAFETY

Fire emergency planning is especially important for families with children. A very important precaution is to get and apply the fluorescent window decals that identify children's bedrooms to rescuers. Then consider assigning secondary responsibility for infants and very young toddlers to an older sibling or a neighbor. That way, if the parents are overcome, someone else will immediately look for the child.

When you have small children who may not be able to remember fire drill instructions, you're likely going to have to do the rescuing. On an upper floor you must have some way of getting them to the ground without using the staircase. In short, you must have some way to reach the children from the outside.

By all means, keep a ladder (preferably a light aluminum one) in your garage or somewhere outside your house. It should reach the porch roof and upper story windows. An old knife or a pair of shears tied to the top rung will help cut the window screens.

Teach your children to use the legs of a chair, a shoe, a book, or another object to smash open a window and clear off the jagged edges, if a window cannot be opened. Blankets or other bedding can be thrown over the sill as protection against cuts.

Instruct children in the right way to escape from a window once it's open: first throw a leg over the sill; then back out. Perhaps there is a ledge or porch on which they can await rescue. If not, teach them to drop, rather than jump, from an upper floor window (if it's not too high) by hanging onto the sill by the fingertips and then letting go.

If your second-floor windows have no porch, it would be pru-dent to buy a special fire escape ladder ($30–$40). These hook under the windowsill and extend down the side of the house. There are models that can be stored in a closet and collapsible units that attach to the outside of the house and look like drainpipes. These can be opened only by a latch at the top.

When buying a ladder, make sure it has these features:

- It should be easy to hook over the windowsill (if not permanently installed).
- You should have plenty of support to hold on to while you're getting out of the window.
- The rungs should be supported away from the wall so that you can easily get your feet onto the rungs. (Even a rope with knots every 12 inches tied to a strong bracket under the sill can save lives.)

If you have no porch or ladder, at least train the children to lean out the window and yell. By leaning out far enough, they will get oxygen and escape the smoke and deadly gases.

PRACTICE, PREVENTION, AND PRECAUTIONS

Practice getting out of the house in different kinds of situations. For example, for a fire in the kitchen everyone would use the front door. Think of other locations where fires may start and plan the best evacuation tactics.

A fire extinguisher is a good investment. One on the second floor is handy for small upstairs blazes. You also need one in the kitchen. In a survey of 200 fire chiefs it was found that out of 40,000 outbreaks fought in one year, almost one-third were handled with fire extinguishers alone.

Be sure to familiarize yourself with the workings of your extinguisher *before* you need to use it: read instructions carefully and thoroughly.

Be sure to buy an extinguisher that can handle three types of fires: (1) paper, wood, draperies, and upholstery; (2) flaming liquids, such as grease and gasoline; and (3) electrical fires. Check your unit once a year.

It also helps if you have a garden hose that will reach any room in the house and keep it handy. Fire captains believe that such a hose could take care of eight out of ten small home fires. Spigots should be placed at two corners of the house.

Inform any overnight guests of your fire escape plan. Tell the baby-sitter about the escape plan and the procedures to follow. If you have a regular baby-sitter, let him or her participate in a drill.

Many lives are lost when rescuers return to a burning house to rescue members of the family who are already outside. Prearrange a meeting place outside the house where all occupants will gather.

Call the fire department only from a neighbor's house.

Also make plans for surviving in the worst kind of winter weather outdoors with very little clothing. Your one great salvation in such circumstances is your car—so keep your car

keys where you can easily find them in an emergency. Keeping a duplicate set in the garage rafters may also be a good idea. Keep the driveway clear and the car in good working order. Thus, when you and your family escape the burning house, the car will give you temporary shelter from the cold.

To lessen the risk of fires, ask the fire department to inspect your home for fire hazards during fire prevention week.

Since three or four minutes can mean the difference between life and death in a fire, automatic fire detection and warning system devices in your home will give you a chance to survive a fire by waking you up promptly. Smoke detectors react to fires faster than heat detectors.

The placement of a detection device is of primary importance. The number of smoke or fire alarms you need for basic protection depends on the size and layout of the house. A sample installation in a two-story house would be one unit in each of the following locations: near the heating plant in the basement, at the top of the stairway to the second floor, and in the attic.

Guidance in the selection and installation of detectors and alarms can be obtained from the National Fire Protection Association in its *Standard for Household Fire Warning Equipment* (NFPA No. 74, available from National Fire Protection Association, Battery March Park, Quincy, MA 02169).

FORGET THE HEROICS

Fire spreads a thousand times faster than you realize. Respect it. And respect the smoke and gases that fire releases. Forget the heroics of saving valuables—save lives instead. Make a floor plan and practice all alternate escape routes. Rehearse procedures often, perhaps every six months. Keep this book handy so you can review this chapter.

Special help is needed for infants, toddlers, the elderly, and the disabled. Have you made a plan? Consult the local fire department for help. Select a meeting place outside. Have the car keys handy. Summon the fire department only when you are all outside.

MORE INFORMATION

For additional information on fire safety, write to the following sources.

- American Insurance Association, Engineering & Safety Service, 85 John St., New York, NY 10038
- National Safety Council, 425 N. Michigan Ave., Chicago, IL 60611
- National Fire Protection Association, 470 Atlantic Ave., Boston, MA 02210

Teaching Children to Be Safe

Doctors give children inoculations to help prevent measles, mumps, and whooping cough. There's no vaccine against danger, but we can help protect our children from accidents that can be just as dangerous as any disease by educating them and ourselves about safety.

One rainy afternoon three-year-old Wendy and her mother were home together. First Wendy asked if she could help cook pancakes. Her mother replied that it was too dangerous because the oil might splatter and burn her.

Then Wendy wanted to make paper dolls. Again her mother said she couldn't because she might cut herself.

Finally, Mother denied Wendy's request to help her use disinfectant on the bathroom floor.

Wendy's mother might have continued to tell her that such things were too dangerous if she hadn't overheard Wendy yelling at her doll, "No, you can't do anything today. Everything's too dangerous and you might get hurt!"

It was then that Wendy's mother realized she could teach

Wendy safety principles by methods other than lecturing and without producing fears or tears.

Wendy's mother decided that her daughter might feel less rejected and more important if she talked to her about potential dangers instead of chasing her away with a "no."

For example, she decided that maybe they could make paper dolls. She showed Wendy the proper way to hold the scissors and let her practice by cutting newspapers. She praised Wendy for small accomplishments and tried to criticize as little as possible. The two were able to discuss the correct method of holding the scissors—sharp end down—while walking.

Then Mother drew and cut out paper dolls for Wendy to play with. This made their discussion of scissor safety a happy and rewarding experience for both.

When Wendy asked again about making pancakes, her mother still felt that splattering oil was too much of a burn hazard for a three-year-old. Instead, she allowed Wendy to help her by getting out the necessary ingredients and mixing them.

Sometimes parents try to protect young children from every problem. If someone was hurt in an accident or fire, they do not want to frighten the child by talking about it. However, an honest and nonfrightening discussion can be a valuable lesson in safety.

Three-year-old Michael was awakened in the middle of the night by the loud sirens of a fire engine. He asked his mother what the noise was. She had seen the fire engine stop at a neighbor's house, but was afraid Michael would have nightmares if she told him the truth. So she said the fire engine was testing its siren.

The next day Michael learned that one of the children in the house had been badly burned. The fire was caused by a cigarette and the house did not have a smoke detector. Michael's mother explained these things to her son.

This discussion led to the family making a plan for escape in case of fire. They ordered "Tot Finder" stickers from their fire department and put them on Michael's window.

They devised a game with Michael. In the game, they pretended there was a fire and practiced their escape plans. After

some initial fear, Michael became secure when he realized how prepared his family was.

A parent and child can talk about safety less directly by using dolls or puppets. This is especially useful when confrontation with the child has led to arguments.

Four-year-old Jenny balked at sitting in her car seat, especially since her older sister used only a seat belt. Mother first tried to persuade Jenny, then threatened. But Jenny continued to refuse.

Finally, Mother took Jenny's Raggedy Ann and Raggedy Andy dolls and played a game. Andy and Ann, Jenny's mother said, were going for a ride. Andy climbed into his car seat, but Ann didn't want to. As they rode along, the car had to stop suddenly. Andy remained safe, but Ann lurched forward and complained of a bad stomachache. For several months thereafter Jenny sat in her car seat, often with the Raggedy Ann doll.

This safety game can be played even with young preschoolers. Make two sets of cards. Draw or paste magazine pictures of safety do's and don'ts on them.

For example, one card might have a picture of toys left on the stairs. One might show a child playing with matches. A third might show a child holding a parent's hand and crossing the street at the corner.

Three cards can be dealt at a time. Each time a player gets a "do" card, he puts it in his pile. The player with the most do's wins.

Another possibility is to use the cards to tell a safety story. Even better, let the child tell the story.

It can be very exciting for a three-to-five-year-old to visit a firehouse, see a fire engine, and hear the firefighters tell about their job. Children also learn some simple safety tips at both fire and police stations.

Finally, children should be encouraged to survey their own houses to make a checklist of potential safety hazards and methods for removing the hazards. While each apartment or house will be different, the following are some general hints for improved safety.

SAFETY MEASURES IN THE HOME

General Safety

- Keep a first-aid kit handy. Keep emergency information posted, especially in the kitchen. Tape emergency numbers near the telephone. Include the numbers of a doctor, hospital, ambulance, and poison control center, among others.
- Be certain stairs are not cluttered. Carpets should be well-anchored and lighting adequate. Safety gates should be placed at the top and the bottom of stairs. Floors should not be slippery.
- If windows are open, they should be open on top or have a screen so a young child cannot climb or fall out. A child should never be allowed to sit on a windowsill.

- Keep all electrical cords flat on the ground and, where possible, tuck them behind couches, chairs, or other objects where they are less likely to be stepped on. Use safety plugs to prevent children from sticking their fingers into the plug area.

Children's Possessions

- Make sure toys are durable and use toys appropriate for the age of the child.

Specific Safety Problems

- *Suffocation.* Plastic bags should be kept out of reach of infants and young children because such bags can cause death by suffocation.
- *Eating.* Children should be taught the proper way to eat, including not running with food in the mouth and eating food in small bites. Adults should know how to remove trapped food and how to aid choking victims.
- *Poisoning.* Childproof locks should be used on all cabinets containing cleaning fluids, laundry detergents, and other poisons.

Cleaning agents should be kept in their original containers. While a child may understand that cleaning fluids should not be drunk, he or she could easily be tempted to drink the contents of a soda bottle.

All medicines should be kept out of reach of children, and antidotes to use in case of poison should be readily available. Medicine should never be treated as candy.

Burn and Fire Safety

- *Smoke Detectors.* Put smoke detectors on each level of your home. Check them regularly (about once a month). Keep fire extinguishers in the kitchen and in rooms where there are wood- or coal-burning stoves or fireplaces.

Make an emergency exit fire plan and practice it.

Car Safety

- Make the car seat attractive by attaching soft toys or teething rings for infants. For toddlers, use dolls, stuffed animals, or small toys. Give toddlers a goody bag on longer trips, containing snacks, crayons and paper, and toys.

When potential hazards are discovered and corrected, and when children are taught safety in a positive way, they will be "inoculated" against danger. Everyone will be happier . . . and safer.

Childhood Fear: Sources and Expressions

Sue and Jim left a lively dinner party early again. The sitter called to tell them that eight-year-old Jenny was still awake and crying at 9:30, insisting that her stomach ached "just terrible" and she was afraid to go to sleep. Now Jenny is sound asleep following some cuddling and a cup of warm cocoa, and Sue and Jim have had an unpleasant scene. A similar incident has happened three times in recent weeks. Jim thinks Jenny is behaving like a spoiled child.

Mary has almost decided to give up trying to go to her weekly morning coffee hour for young mothers. The mothers have a planned discussion hour while the children play together in another room, but four-year-old Tommy won't stay with the other children. If Mary leaves in spite of his crying, he wails louder and louder and ends up vomiting all over the place. Leaving him is getting worse instead of better. Yesterday he cried when she left him with a neighbor friend while she ran to the store. His pitiful "Mommy, don't leave me" seemed to carry genuine fear and despair.

Children's fears have countless expressions and countless sources. This chapter will sort out some of these sources and examine how fears are expressed.

We will begin by grouping fears into three general classifications: fear of abandonment, fear of the unknown, and fear of specific objects or events.

FEAR OF ABANDONMENT

Perhaps the most basic of all human fears is the fear of abandonment. There is a sense in which we never completely outgrow that fear. Have you stood waiting for a ride on a street corner darkening by the minute, realized you must have been forgotten, and felt that sinking feeling?

The fear of abandonment arises very early. Around six months the infant begins to realize that the caregiver is sometimes not available to him either physically or psychologically, and because of the state of an infant's mental development, at

first this absence is felt as permanent. With experience the infant learns that the caregiver returns and he develops trust that his caregiver will not go away forever.

If for some reason the mother (or other primary caregiver) must be away for an extended period of time while the child is learning to count on her return, he may become "stuck" in his fear of abandonment to some degree. Other difficulties in early childhood may also be tied into the fear of abandonment and possibly surface in disguised form.

FEAR OF THE UNKNOWN

Most of us remember very little about our preschool years and cannot tap our own experiences to judge whether our preschooler feels as we felt at that age. But forgotten or not, it is likely that fear occupied a very large part of our emotional world then. There are fears of imaginary monsters, of the dark, of strange places and faces, even of commonplace events that seem quite ordinary to adults. A rapidly developing imagination (a healthy sign of a maturing mind) is the biggest source of a toddler's fears. Unreasonable but very real, the child may live in terror of a monster he made up.

FEARS OF NATURAL EVENTS, ACCIDENTS, CRIMES

Another set of childhood fears involves happenings in the world in which he lives. Even though young children cannot read, they are exposed to television news, bulletins, and warnings. Our children are therefore aware of the tragedies and crimes that have always been a part of living. Generally speaking, such events were not discussed in front of young children in previous generations, and probably most families still do not talk about child molesting, train wrecks, mangled bodies, or painfully slow death by cancer in front of their little children. But the children see all this and more on a daily basis if they watch TV indiscriminately. Even a carefully chosen child's program may be interrupted by tornado warnings or news of yet another assassination, including graphic color pictures of a dying president.

The child may develop an unbalanced picture of the frequency or immediacy of such events and become very fearful of the world. To her it may come to seem a very dangerous place. Her generalized fear may become attached to a specific hazard such as a dog she must pass on the way to school, or it may appear as a constant dread that something will happen to her parent while at work. Her wish to keep her mother safe may be expressed in crying and terror when Mom leaves her.

Having identified some common kinds of fears, let us consider some parental responses to them. For the sake of clarity, we will group the responses as we did the fears, but of course you may be responding in more than one way as you meet a particular fear.

IDENTIFY THE FEAR EMOTION

The first response step will be to examine the whole situation in which the child's fear arises.

Because fear is a negative emotion, it is often difficult to accept and very easily becomes confused with other negative emotions such as anger, loneliness, and grief. If you can identify the underlying emotion and deal with it, the fear may go away.

In addition, emotions in the parent may be triggering emotions in the child, which come out as fear. Let's go back to the illustrations with which we began the chapter to see how this works.

Sue and Jim are a young professional couple, both successfully working upward in satisfying careers. They agreed that they wanted to have the parenting experience as well, and both are delighted with Jenny. Over the years they have made good arrangements for child care for Jenny, and she seems to be a healthy, emotionally serene little girl.

However, Jim's latest promotion has meant more social evenings out, and Sue feels quite guilty about being gone so many evenings on top of fulfilling the requirements of her daytime job.

Jenny is feeling a little lonely but is also quite proud of her busy mother and has never directly asked her to stay home with her. But her stomach really did hurt, and it was nice of Mother to come home when she really needed her. Mother has always managed to get home from work, too, when she was sick.

In this illustration there is guilt and role confusion for Sue, which needs to be discussed and dealt with between Sue and Jim. There is also loneliness and perhaps jealousy in Jenny, which her parents should handle with Jenny.

In our second example Mary is completely puzzled by Tommy's growing unwillingness to be separated from her. She is not a particularly expressive person but prides herself on handling difficult situations well.

Her mother died of cancer three months ago, and Mary welcomed her into their home and cared for her lovingly until the last few days of her life. She herself drove her mother to the hospital for the last time, leaving Tommy with a neighbor. She has talked very little to anyone about her grief over her mother's painful death, and her explanation to Tommy was "Grandma has gone away."

Our example suggests that Mary must come to terms with her own emotional response to her mother's death. Then she will be able to recognize the source of Tommy's fear and offer him adequate comfort and explanations regarding the loss of his grandmother. When, as in this case, the child's fear seems to be the fear of abandonment, he must learn that his mother will come back, and this will take time and patience. The lesson is learned not because the caregiver is always there, but because the caregiver always returns. Frequent short absences will help Tommy depend again on Mary's return.

As you examine the child's situation and apparently unrelated events in the life of the whole family, you may come to understand how a child's fear fits in with your own emotions. Once identified, you can begin to deal with underlying distress, sadness, anger, guilt, etc., in yourself or in the child.

Sometimes events outside the home are the source of the

child's fear, so you must look at those situations as well as you attempt to identify the fear accurately. Perhaps an older child is relentlessly teasing the child. The teacher may be setting standards so high that the child cannot meet them. The grandmother may have an extraordinary fear of storms, which the child notices. The overly imaginative baby-sitter may be planting fears with wild stories. Because the child wishes to be thought competent and strong (goals constantly set before him) he may not confide the specific problem to his parent, and the fear may surface in some less readily recognized form.

Occasionally a very conscientious parent trying to do a good job is the unwitting source of generalized fearfulness in the child. The parent may hover too closely over the child, issuing a stream of warnings: "Don't hurry; you'll trip. Look again. You'll get hit by a car. Don't play with sticks. You might poke your eye out," etc. etc. The child hears this constant stream of warnings, internalizes them, and begins to issue them to himself even when his mother is not around. Try to frame necessary instructions to young children in encouraging terms rather than threatening ones. Remember that if you have a worried, fearful outlook on the world, your child may copy it.

LOWER THE GENERAL STRESS LEVEL

A second response to your child's fear may involve a general change in her life. A child may become fearful and attach the fear to a specific object or event because the general level of tension and uncertainty in her life is too high. In this situation, try to provide a more stable routine the child can depend on. The sense of knowing what will happen next—predictability in his life—will help allay fearfulness.

Also, try to avoid overloading your child with responsibility or decision-making duties. A retreat into "babyish" fearfulness may be his way of letting you know that he does not feel ready to handle emergencies if left alone in the house. Try to match your requirements to his sense of being comfortably able to handle them.

MODIFY THE EXTERNAL SOURCES OF FEARS

Following the earlier suggestion to make careful observation of the child's situation may make you aware of some previously unnoticed sources of fear, and you may decide you need to modify some of these sources. For example, one time our young son became extremely preoccupied and fearful about weather reports and tornadoes. Until we watched the weather warnings with him, we did not realize how wide a band of weather information the channel he was watching covered. He had been getting warnings about tornadoes that were unlikely to come near us, but since his sense of geography was very undeveloped, he did not know that.

We drew a big map, located our city and the television station on it, and helped him see which place names he needed to be concerned about. He was still very conscientious about tornado warnings, but at least he did not worry about tornadoes hundreds of miles away.

Other TV broadcasts may be frightening your child. I assume you are already aware of and supervise the content of programs your children watch. In addition, much of the evening news probably is not suitable for daily viewing by the young child.

Evidence suggests that older people who watch more TV have a greater fearfulness of being mugged in the streets than similar people living in the same neighborhood who watch less television. Perhaps your child is getting a distorted view of how often crimes or violent accidents actually happen.

It may be helpful to show him how many pages in your local paper are about school events, weddings, sports, and other ordinary affairs so that he has a more accurate picture of what is happening. By its nature, television coverage tends to be graphic and emotional in tone, especially for the young child who ignores the commentator and "reads" the pictures. Try to encourage your child's interest in printed news.

In a commendable attempt to use the media to reach and warn children and adults many commercials of today discuss child molesters, dangers to children who run away, cancer signals, and a host of other public service messages. Most are not understandable to the young child and may increase her fears rather than help her, unless interpreted by adults.

TALK TO YOUR CHILD ABOUT FEAR AS AN EMOTION

Explain to your child in his language the physiology of fear. Help him know that being afraid is one of the ways his body prepares to deal with real danger.

It is important for your child to know that fear is an acceptable human emotion that can be recognized, admitted, and managed constructively.

RESPECT YOUR CHILD'S PERSONALITY

Some children seem to be born challenging the whole world to a fight; others are timid and peace-loving. Some children have a vivid, creative imagination; others never conjure up anything scary. It probably will not help a shy or timid child to push her into strange situations unprepared. The imaginary monsters your child creates will not disappear for her because you say they are not real. Warmth, reassurance, and a genuine respect for your child as she now is will go a long way toward helping her cope with her fears.

Fears are a normal part of childhood, and learning to handle fear is part of a child's emotional development. Help your child accurately recognize his fears, locate their sources, plan ways to handle them, accept himself the way he is. With your loving, intelligent support, your child will put fear into perspective and use this feeling toward the goal of emotional maturity.

Childhood Fear (Part Two): How to Help Children Overcome Fear

All of us, even as adults, have been frightened—of snakes, spiders, strange noises, dark rooms, death.

Many of our fears are common; as adults we can usually handle or forget them. But children are not like adults:

- They can't always distinguish fantasy from reality.
- They don't have mature reasoning skills.
- And they haven't had many opportunities to cope with fear.

You can, however, help your child overcome fears. Talking about fears at your child's level of understanding—in his or her own language—can be an invaluable source of information and comfort. Openly discussing fears will reassure your child that having fears is a very normal part of growing up.

THE DEVELOPMENT OF FEARS IN CHILDREN

Fears in childhood are normal; many are even helpful. You

want your child to develop a healthy fear of strangers, sharp knives, and busy highways. But you also want to help your child overcome fears of irrational or unrealistic dangers.

There is a big difference between normal fears that almost all children experience and irrational or persistent fears that may inhibit a child's growth toward independence.

At birth most infants are afraid of loud noises, sudden movements, and abrupt changes in surroundings. Almost all children grow out of these innate fears as they explore their environments and become more independent.

Within the first year infants develop fears of strangers and of separation. Distressful responses to strangers are very common from seven to fifteen months and may last a year or two.

At about age three children often develop symbolic and imagined fears. Growth in reasoning skills—along with repeated experiences—will eventually put these fears out of mind.

Imitation may also affect a child's fears. Parents, siblings, or others a child sees frequently may be frightened of thunderstorms, spiders, or airplanes and may convey the same fears to the child. Children may also develop fears based on their own experiences. Two-year-old Mary is jostled when a dog upsets her playpen and becomes afraid of all dogs. She may even associate the dog with all furry animals and be frightened of cats, rabbits, and hampsters as well. Although fears of these kinds, like natural, developmental fears, often disappear with age, it is helpful for parents to recognize and help children overcome them.

RECOGNIZING FEAR IN CHILDREN

What can you do to recognize fear in your child and help him or her to overcome it? An infant may cry loudly and exhibit a startle response—arms thrust outward, body rigid—when frightened.

Older children's reactions are more varied. Children may run, cling, scream, close their eyes, freeze in panic in a frightening situation; it is easy to recognize that these children are afraid. But the child who shows an exaggerated fascination with spiders—for example, constantly asking questions about them and always looking for them—may be just as worried as a child who exhibits obviously fearful behavior.

When does a child's fear become so exaggerated that it is maladaptive, preventing normal growth toward independence? Sandy may be afraid to go walking in the woods because she may see a snake. That is not unusual. But if she is afraid to go out of the house because she may see a snake in the yard or in the street, she has developed an exaggerated fear that prevents growth toward self-confidence and independence.

If you suspect that your child has a persistent or maladaptive fear, talk with adults who see your child in other situations—a nursery school teacher, another parent in the neighborhood. Does your child exhibit this fear at nursery school or with playmates? Can you or other familiar adults talk with your child about the fear?

HELPING YOUR CHILD WITH FEAR

Many fears will disappear naturally as your child's reasoning and mental capabilities increase. Infant fears of unfamiliar objects and persons disappear early; preschool fears of imaginary creatures gradually give way to concrete, realistic concerns about school, pain, injury, illness, and death. Even some fears intense enough to be labeled phobias disappear because of developmental growth. You can, however, help your child cope with the fears of childhood by using the following techniques.

- Talk with your child about his fears; communication can be a source of information, comfort, and encouragement. Instead of ridiculing a child by saying, "It's silly to be afraid of the cat," encourage the child to talk about feelings and perceptions by saying, "If you feel scared, talk to me about it."

  You can also help your child by talking about your own feelings: "Yes, dark rooms sometimes frighten me, too. Here's what I do to feel less scared." In any case, encouraging your child to talk about sensitive subjects in general

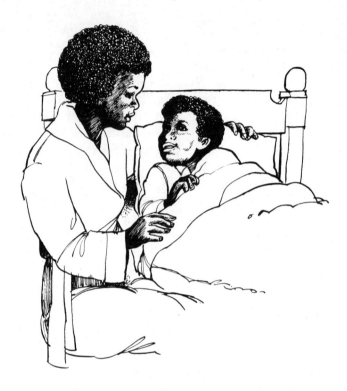

will provide an atmosphere that is conducive to talking about fears.

- Give your child accurate information about fears; do not use confusing or fear-producing explanations to establish obedience with your child. If you explain death as a long, long sleep, your child may be terrified of going to bed at night. Or saying, "You'll have to go to the doctor and get a shot if you don't behave," may increase your child's fear of doctors.

- Select good children's books about fears to read with your child. Books about children's fears can provide honest information and clarify misinformation your child may have picked up. They can assure your child that she is not the only one experiencing fear, give her the opportunity to see others handling fear and to rehearse different solutions to the problem, and allow her to think and talk about the feelings of a story character when it is too painful to talk about her own feelings or fear.

- Use art and puppets to help your child verbalize feelings about fear. After your child paints or draws a picture or constructs a scene with clay, ask him to tell you a story based on the artwork.

  You can encourage further discussion about the fear which expression through art has now made less painful. It is also easier for a child to voice threatening or confusing thoughts with a puppet, because it is the puppet, rather than the child, who is expressing the fear. The puppet says, "I hate doctors. They hurt me!" The puppet asks, "When is my Daddy coming back? I miss him." Particularly for the child who doesn't want to admit fear, puppets provide an opportunity to examine reality, rehearse solutions, express emotions, and gain mastery over the situation. This imaginative play can help a child learn to deal with a scary situation through repeated rehearsals in fantasy; the next time the scary situation is confronted "for real" it will be easier to face.

- Broaden your child's range of skills for coping with fear. Help your child identify her potential strengths. Ask your child, "What do you think would help you when you are afraid of the dark?" Knowing that she has options available will make your child feel more powerful and in control over fearful situations.

  Play the game "What if?" with your child: "What if you got lost?" "What if it started to storm?" "What if the lights went out?" Children who realize that they are resourceful and can do something about frightening situations are better able to overcome their fears.

All of us have experienced fear. And as sensitive, caring parents, we want to protect our children from fearful situations. But we cannot always protect our children, nor can we keep them from being afraid. We can, however, reduce our children's fearfulness by helping them express their fears, distinguish real from imaginary dangers, and become increasingly independent and confident about handling frightening situations they encounter as they mature.

WHEN YOUR CHILD IS AFRAID

- Talk with your child about the frightening situation. Let your child know that he can talk with you about anything—even sensitive subjects. Don't create an atmosphere in which your child feels guilty or ashamed if he brings up a touchy subject.
- Allow your child plenty of time to talk over fears. Don't push your child into a scary situation. Forcing her to stay in a dark room will only intensify the fear of the dark.
- Accept your child's fears, feelings, and reactions. Don't deny what your child is fearing; these fears are very real to her. Ridiculing or shaming your child will make her hide her feelings from you.
- Tell your child the truth about frightening events. "Yes, the shot needle may hurt you. So it's OK to yell and make faces, but you need to hold still." Don't deceive your child about stressful or frightening events. Providing information about the hospital (or death or divorce) isn't harmful to your child; deceiving him is.
- Involve your child in decision making and problem solving about frightening situations to enhance his feelings of power and competence. Ask, "What do you think would help a child who is afraid?"
- Give your child books to read about other children experiencing fear. And let your child use art and puppet play to express feelings and rehearse solutions to frightening situations.
- Suggest ways your child can cope with fears: "Some people who are afraid of the dark carry a flashlight or use a nightlight. What would make you feel better?" Don't limit your child's options for adaptive behaviors by emphasizing the negatives: "Don't cry!" "Don't act like a baby!" Instead, suggest what your child can do.

CHILDREN'S BOOKS ABOUT FEAR

These books for children of ages three to eight show ways children overcome various childhood fears.

Iwasaki, Chihiro. *Staying Home Alone on a Rainy Day.* New York: McGraw-Hill, 1968.

Mahy, Margaret. *A Lion in the Meadow.* New York: Franklin Watts, 1969.

Mayer, Mercer. *You're the Scaredy-Cat.* New York: Parents' Magazine Press, 1974.

———. *There's a Nightmare in my Closet.* New York: The Dial Press, 1968.

Sonneborn, Ruth. *The Lollipop Party.* New York: Viking, 1967.

Viorst, Judith. *My Momma Says There Aren't Any Zombies, Ghosts, Vampires, Creatures, Demons, Monsters, Fiends, Goblins, or Things.* New York: Atheneum, 1973.

Waber, Bernard. *Ira Sleeps Over.* Boston: Houghton Mifflin Company, 1972.

Watson, Jane. *Sometimes I'm Afraid.* Racine, WI: Western Publishing Co., Inc., 1971.

BOOKS FOR PARENTS ABOUT CHILDREN'S FEARS

Franger, Richard. *Your Child From One to Six.* Washington, DC: Department of Health, Education, and Welfare, 1978 (pages 53 65).

Joseph, Stephen. *Mommy! Daddy! I'm Afraid.* New York: Collier Books, 1974.

Salk, Lee. *Dear Dr. Salk: Answers to Your Questions about Your Family.* New York: Warner Books, Inc., 1979 (pages 209 221).

Wolman, Benjamin. *Children's Fears.* New York: Grosset and Dunlap, 1978.

Child Abuse: Why It Happens, How to Prevent It

Child abuser! The name calls up instant distaste and a violent reaction. Even in prisons, where many labels of our society are ignored, this one generates special hatred. No one wants to be called a child abuser.

But just what is child abuse?

A mother writes, "I get angry with my children. Sometimes I react to their behavior in ways I wish I hadn't. Sometimes I witness behavior toward children in the homes of friends and relatives that worries or embarrasses me. Is this child abuse?"

It is difficult to find a precise definition that everyone agrees on. A broad definition might include any action that is detrimental to a child's development or any action that causes a child long-term physical, emotional, intellectual, or spiritual damage.

In this chapter we are primarily going to discuss physical violence directed toward a child. This violence may be intentional as part of discipline or unintentional because the child happens to be present when violence erupts in the family.

We will discuss the framework in which child abuse tends to occur, point out places in the family system where help can be offered, and suggest changes that will reduce the incidences of abuse.

POTENTIAL FOR ABUSE

Studies show that everyone is a potential child abuser. A mother writes: "I . . . have occasionally had fleeting feelings of violence toward the child I love more than anything else in the world. Once, while changing my baby's diaper, he kicked and squirmed and wiggled so much, and I was in a hurry and short of patience, that for an instant I had a strong violent urge to stab the baby in the thigh with the diaper pin! The feeling was gone in a flash, but just the fact that I had felt it shocked me. The potential for child abuse was there."

Child abuse happens in all social, economic, religious and ethnic groups. Child abusers are usually closely related to the child—a parent, stepparent, or other caregiver. They are just ordinary people, up against problems or situations they don't feel able to cope with. All parents are potential child abusers, in fact, because all parents are subject to stress and frustration—two major factors leading to violence against children.

STRESS

Stress comes from events in our daily lives, our environments, and our relationships and interaction with others. According to one mother, stress is the "nonspecific response of the body to any demand made upon it." In other words, any time you have to make some kind of adjustment because of something that's happened to you that event is stressful. Stress has also been defined as the perception of a threat to physical or psychological well-being and the feeling of being inadequate to cope with it.

FRUSTRATION

Stress leads to frustration, which results when we're blocked from an anticipated goal. We may be frustrated when we don't get a job promotion we expected or when our child just can't seem to stay dry at night, in spite of our efforts.

Let's look at some situations in which stress and frustration can lead to abuse.

A mother of four, ages two, four, six, and nine, is usually a calm, pleasant, intelligent, loving person. Sometimes, though, she gets very angry and frustrated with the four little ones, the large house, the husband who works long and irregular hours, and the fact that she can't easily get away because it's hard to find a sitter for so many children. She says that's when she spanks a child too hard or resorts to yelling much too frequently.

A father is reprimanded at work. He worries about the effect the reprimand will have on his job and his ability to do the work. The more he thinks about it, the angrier he becomes that he didn't defend himself. But out of fear for his job, he says nothing. At home that evening he berates his wife or hits his child.

OTHER WAYS OF RESPONDING

We learn as infants that we cannot always have things exactly as we would like them, and we find ways to make the best of that fact. The child who is left alone may cry very loudly for her mother. If her mother comes back, the stress is relieved and the frustration at being alone goes away.

If Mother does not come back, the child can learn to handle that frustration positively by playing happily alone. On the other hand, the frustration may turn to anger and result in quarrels or tantrums—a negative response.

Something similar happens to adults. When something happens that you don't like (stress), and your efforts to change it don't work (frustration), you can react either positively or negatively.

There are ways to break the stress-frustration-abuse cycle:

- Lower the stress.
- Find better ways to cope with frustration.
- Release the frustration in ways that don't hurt children.

Let's look at each of these goals and suggest concrete methods that have helped formerly abusive parents.

IDENTIFYING AND LOWERING STRESS

The first goal is to lower stress levels in the parent and in the family. We are all different, so what bothers you may not affect your neighbor. To deal with stress you first need to identify your individual sources of stress. Either alone, with your spouse, or with a friend, make a list of your stress sources. Below are some possibilities to get your list started.

Sources of Stress

- Feelings of fear or inadequacy about child-rearing abilities
- Feelings of resentment or trouble in relationships with family or spouse
- Poor health, alcoholism, drug abuse
- Feelings of sadness, depression, loneliness
- Day-to-day routine of caring for a child
- Difficulty with premature, sickly, handicapped, or hard-to-handle child
- Job worries
- Money problems
- Sick or aging parents
- Crowded housing, unsafe neighborhood

Stress doesn't always have negative sources. Planning a wedding, squeezing in an extra vacation, getting a job promotion, or choosing new furniture can also be stressful.

TAKING CHARGE OF STRESS SOURCES

With your list of stress sources in hand, you are ready to take charge of them.

Which ones can be eliminated? For example, do you really need that second job? Could the budget be managed if you worked fewer hours? Do the children need clean clothes from the skin out every day, or could you cut the laundry work with some cooperation from the family?

How about your ability to manage the child-rearing task? Is there a class for parents where you could learn some skills and at the same time get encouragement and support?

As you look at each source of stress, be as creative as possible about ways to lower the stress from that source. Don't accept the way things are until you have explored even the most far-out kind of solution.

A family service worker, a homemaker's consultant, a child guidance worker, an experienced mother in the neighborhood, or a good friend can help you with ideas. Don't play "Yes, but": "Yes, but it won't work." "Yes, but this or that." The decision to take charge of the sources of stress in your life is a good one. Act on that decision!

HANDLING FRUSTRATION

Your list of stress sources will be shortened by trying some creative ways of dealing with or eliminating them. But it's impossible to get rid of all stress; all of us have to live with some frustration.

We develop characteristic ways to handle frustration when we are relatively young, and these patterns tend to persist through adulthood. Some negative patterns are:

- lashing out at others;
- berating ourselves;
- withdrawing from people;
- sleeping and eating more than we need.

Positive patterns include:

- engaging in hard physical activity;
- seeking new sources of satisfaction (friends, hobbies, activities);
- adapting old behaviors to our new circumstances.

With the help of a friend, counselor, or spouse, try to analyze how you handle the large and small frustrations of life.

Even if your habitual patterns are poor, you are not stuck with them. Once you recognize your patterns you are in a position to substitute a positive reaction for any negative ones.

Changing the way you react to frustration may be difficult, but you can do it. Having friends for support is important. It is a good idea to hunt up a parent group to join. Call social services, a city church, Family Services, or the school counselor to help you find one. Your goal is to learn to handle stress and frustration in ways that reduce the tension and allow positive results.

ELIMINATING VIOLENCE

It is an unfortunate fact that many of us have learned to respond to frustration with violence. We have stored many memories of adults who were violent, and it may seem natural to hit when certain situations occur. A personal campaign to eliminate child abuse in our homes may have to include a decision to forego violence as the solution to child-rearing problems.

Some child abuse is deliberate in the sense that the parent really believes hurting the child is the best way to change his behavior. Actually, while hurting the child may stop the behavior, it provides no instruction for what the child should be doing and certainly doesn't teach good behavior. Parents may begin hitting the child more often and harder, telling themselves it is for the child's own good.

There are many ways to respond to behavior other than hitting. Other parents, parenting classes, magazine articles, and books are sources of new ideas in child management. Some parents have found that a time-out chair for the child gives both parent and child a chance to think through the situation.

Some violence against children occurs just because the child happens to be in the way when an adult is feeling frustrated. The source of the frustration may be unrelated to the child. The adult needs to learn to handle stress in other ways—for example, noncompetitive exercise like walking, jogging, or swimming; hobbies; or time spent alone. Each person needs to find alternatives that work.

In the meantime the child may need to be out of the way while the parent works out the underlying problem. Many a child has made the sensible decision not to bother Mom and Dad when they just came in from rush-hour traffic! More complicated strategies may be needed to remove the younger child or teach him to remove himself.

IF A CHILD IS BEING ABUSED

Sometimes when child abuse has already begun a cycle has been established in which the abuse itself becomes a source of stress. While isolated incidents of child abuse sometimes do great harm, repeated abuse is even more destructive to a child's growth and personality. Intervention is needed to stop the abuse, and early intervention works best.

If you need help, ask for it. You're not a bad parent if you sometimes feel you can't cope. When you feel that way, though, try to put into practice the principles outlined in this article or reach out to some other adult rather than lash out at your child.

If you know of someone else who is being abusive, you may be able to help him or her using these principles of stress management. If you cannot, try to have the person get other outside help. If he or she will not, you can report the situation to child protection authorities. You may be the child's only hope.

CALLING CHILD ABUSE TELEPHONE HOT LINES

Most people want to know what will happen when they call a child abuse telephone hot line or child protection agency— before they dial the number.

The purpose of a child abuse telephone hot line is to reach out to parents who are troubled and who have not sought help elsewhere for fear of being treated harshly by professionals, authorities, friends, or relatives. The person who answers the telephone will probably ask a few preliminary questions but will not demand your name unless you choose to give it.

A telephone hot line provides an atmosphere in which the caller can remain anonymous and can discuss problems openly and freely. Staffers are trained to handle calls from parents and others who may be at the end of their rope or who just need another adult to talk to. They will listen without cutting you off or shutting you out. They will try to hear what you are saying and feeling without judging you.

There are two toll-free national telephone hot lines:

1-800-423-5805
1-800-421-0353

Locally, look in the telephone directory yellow pages for organizations with the words *family, parents, child,* or *children* in them. Look for programs with names like *family service agency* or *parental stress hot line* or *family stress center.* The local mental health organization may also be a good place to start.

When a Child Is Being Abused

If a child is actually being abused, the case will be referred to a worker who will investigate in as nonthreatening a manner as possible. The intent is to offer help and prevent further harm to the child. Except in urgent cases, the child will not be removed from the home, since this is likely to do more harm than good in the long run.

Types of Intervention

Every situation is different, and communities are trying different kinds of intervention geared to resources in the community, the type of abuse, and the needs of the parents. A typical intervention program includes the following factors, adapted to a particular family's needs.

1. Medical evaluation of the child and gathering of as much factual information as available and needed
2. Enlistment of the parent in a plan to help

3. Evaluation of the way the whole family is functioning and development of a treatment plan that medical people, social workers, and family all agree on
4. Enrollment of parents in parent workshops with other families also in treatment programs
5. Provision of parent aides or homemakers to help families in the home on an individual basis
6. Help with practical problems of the family as necessary— income, housing, food, care for handicapped children, and so forth
7. Ongoing support, evaluation, and eventual discharge of the family from the treatment program as family relationships improve

Whether legal authorities are included in the child abuse prevention program of a community depends on local law. In general, every effort is made to help, not punish, the parent who is abusing a child. If the parent cannot or will not accept help and the child continues to be abused, law enforcement officials will step in.

When a child is being abused, both parent and child need help. If you need help, please ask for it. If you can help another parent, please get involved. Child abuse hurts the child, the parent, and the community as a whole—and all of us must be part of prevention and treatment.

How Close in Age Should Your Children Be?

Young couples have debated the subject of spacing children for many years. The classic positions are as follows: (1) you should have children close together because they will be friends for each other and you'll get the child-rearing process over with quickly; or (2) you should space children several years apart so you won't be overloaded with work.

There are two even more powerful reasons for being concerned with the topic. In research of the last thirteen years on the development of the young child in his own home it has been shown repeatedly that the greatest single source of stress for young families comes when children are spaced close together. The dividing line seems to be about three years; children spaced closer than three years apart clearly cause considerably more stress to themselves and to their parents than those spaced more than three years apart. Furthermore, the closer the spacing, the greater the stress.

The second reason this topic is an important issue is that much more is known now about how children grow and develop, and how they interact with other children. This information can help parents make the decision on a sounder basis and can lead to much better results for all concerned.

THE BASIC FACTS ABOUT SOCIAL DEVELOPMENT

During the first two years of life young humans, like most warm-blooded creatures, must form a strong attachment to at least one older creature. This process has been studied extensively over the last twenty or thirty years, and we think it is now reasonably well understood. All interpersonal relations rest on the attachment that is formed during the first two years of life.

Another characteristic of those first years is that the human's focus on attention is, under most circumstances, primarily in the home. Also during those first two years, babies go from no sense of self to an awareness of themselves as persons. This change begins to occur soon after the first birthday and intensifies during the second year of life. Accompanying the emergence of self-awareness is the routine surfacing of negativism or testing of power that studies indicate begins around the fifteenth month of life and lasts at least through the twenty-first month and often well into the third year. A final comment about those first social developments is that first children and widely spaced children live mostly in warm and accepting social environments.

After the second birthday the situation changes rather dramatically. There is a steady decline in the exclusive focus on the primary person in the home and in the home itself. This exclusive focus is replaced by a divided interest that now includes age mates for the first time. By that I mean that true social interest in children their own age begins to be a real factor in the lives of children past the second birthday. Along with this emergence we find children for the first time facing up to interpersonal difficulties and challenges in situations outside the home. By then, presumably, the child is sturdy enough to be able to withstand some of the minor problems that come along with social disagreements during the third and fourth years and beyond.

CLOSELY SPACED CHILDREN: A ONE-YEAR GAP

Let us move through the first years of life in the situation in which children are very closely spaced. During the first seven months of life a second child with a one-year-older sibling experiences little or no difference in social development as a consequence of having an older sibling. Much time is spent sleeping, and most other time is spent out of the way of the ongoing daily activities of the older child. During these months the baby is immobile and comparatively easy to care for.

The older child will be growing from twelve to nineteen months of age during this time. For such a child the presence of a new baby makes little or no difference even though between fifteen and nineteen months of age the older child is developing a sense of self and personal power and is engaged in the testing of wills with his mother.

When the baby is seven to nine months of age he begins to crawl. A crawling baby requires a good deal of attention if trouble is to be minimized. The older child, in the meantime, is nineteen to twenty-one months of age and really embroiled in negativism; he too has to have his mother's attention, and frequently at that. These equally valid needs simply cannot always both be fulfilled. The older child has to have his mother's attention, but now, rather abruptly, he finds that she is very often busy with baby, in fact too busy for him. This situation leads to the first feelings of jealousy, the first feelings that the world is not perfect, and the first acts of aggression toward the baby. This is the time when you begin to see toys ripped away from an eight-month-old child. This is the time when you begin to see rough treatment of the baby by the older child.

As the younger child grows from nine to twelve months of age he still requires a good deal of attention to minimize accidents and minor damage to the home. The older child, between twenty-one and twenty-four months of age, is very likely under these conditions also to continue to require much attention because the resolution of the issue of who runs the home is likely to have been delayed by the events of the preceding months. The result is that the older child exhibits even more jealousy, more anger, and more resentment toward the baby. The younger child, for his part, has begun to adapt to the increased pace of aggression and hostility from the older child. During this time the younger child learns how useful it is to cry early rather than late. The older child has begun the process of "souring," going from a situation in which the world looked fantastic to one in which he can't quite figure out what's going on, but he knows things aren't good. This, by the way, is a very sad situation to watch.

I have used the following type of story to express just how difficult a situation a two-year-old finds himself in when he's living with a ten-month-old younger brother or sister. (This situation can develop regardless of the sex of the children.) He's in the same situation a woman would be in if her husband one day made the following announcement: "Honey, I've got wonderful news for you. Next week I'm planning to bring home someone else to live with us. It'll be a woman; she'll be a bit younger than you, perhaps a bit more attractive. In any event, she'll seem that way because I plan to spend more time with her than with you; nevertheless, we're all going to continue to be a very happy family. You'll get used to her presence, and I very much want you to love her and to show how much you love her."

I believe most young women would have a very difficult time getting used to such a situation. Yet that's pretty much what we're asking a two-year-old to do when there is a newly crawling baby in the same home. If a full-grown woman would find such a situation totally intolerable, how on earth can we expect a two-year-old, whose whole life revolves around the home, and particularly around the central person in the home during the day, to be able to cope with the feelings that result? The answer is that there simply is no way that that can be done. The only two-year-old who wouldn't be extremely jealous and unhappy about the presence of a nine- or ten-month-old sibling would be one who had very little to lose. The only kind of child of two years of age with very little to lose in that sort of situation would be one who had not formed a solid attachment to his own mother. In a sense, then, the nasty behavior of the two-year-old toward the younger sibling is reasonably good proof that the older child has had normal beneficial early attachment experiences and has formed a very strong tie to his mother.

As the younger child grows from twelve to fifteen months of age his position in regard to his older brother is that of being on guard. The older child, just past his second birthday and moving on to twenty-seven months of age, is increasingly unhappy and frustrated. The result, given the survival tactics learned by the younger child in the preceding few months, is a standoff. That situation shifts when the younger child is fifteen to twenty-one months of age and in turn enters into his first awareness of self, testing of wills, and sense of personal power.

The baby is also moving toward the final stages of his own attachment relationship to his mother. The older child, twenty-seven to thirty-four months of age, now may find himself on the defensive at times. Indeed, the younger child sometimes becomes the dominant one of the pair. This is also the age when the souring of the personality of the older child often peaks, and for good reason. Remember that when the older child lashes out at the younger child, on the basis of strong feelings of jealousy, he often finds his mother, the person whose love is central to his security, showing anger toward him. This, of course, makes matters even worse because she is showing him that she just doesn't love him anymore.

If all of this sounds grim, I am sorry. Unfortunately, this sort of situation does occur over and over. You may escape it, as some people do, but if you're planning your family, you should consider preventing such problems. If, on the other hand, you already have two closely spaced children, we hope to be helpful by explaining what's going on and then moving on to whatever advice we can offer. In the meantime, let's turn to the situation in which the gap is more than three years.

CHILDREN MORE THAN THREE YEARS APART

During the first seven months of the second child's life the fact that there is a three-year-old child at home makes little or no difference in social development. Correspondingly, for the older child the early attachment process is old business. Increasingly since his second birthday he has spent more and more time out of his home. He has begun to develop genuine friendships with age mates and, in general, finds that the impact of a new baby on his daily life is very slight. Even when the new baby gets to be seven or nine months of age and is crawling and requiring more of his mother's attention, he still doesn't make much of a dent in the daily activities of the older child, who by then is at least 43 or 45 months old. At three and one-half years of age, the older child doesn't often feel the need to compete with the baby for the attention of his mother. That's not to say it never happens, but it's not nearly as central to his life and to his daily developmental focus as it would be if he were less than two years of age. As a result there is no "nose out of joint" quality in the older child's interaction with the baby. The baby is not seen as a threat; in fact, such older children genuinely seem to enjoy the baby a great deal. The baby, for his part, does not often experience aggression from his older sibling.

DEALING WITH CLOSELY SPACED CHILDREN

Having described the situation in the two cases, what can we recommend to someone who has two closely spaced children?

The first order of business is to be very careful that the older child doesn't do serious harm to the baby; he or she is perfectly capable of it. In fact, at times the older child will want to inflict harm on the baby. This should be regarded as normal though unacceptable behavior.

Second, don't aggravate the difficulty by lavishly praising the younger child in the presence of the older one.

Third, the more out-of home experiences the older child can have, the more depressurization can take place. If the older child, for example, is two and one-half or going on three, a regular play group would be an excellent idea; but, in any event, the use of a baby-sitter and excursions to the park or elsewhere would help. This will provide beneficial contrast to spending twenty-four hours a day in the home with the younger child and the mother.

Finally, of course, it's terribly important for the older child to have undivided attention from either mother or father regularly day after day to reassure the older child in the only language that she can fully understand that she is loved just as much as ever.

To repeat my caveat, there simply is no way to make this situation as easy to live with as if you were dealing with a first child only or with widely spaced children. It is very important that both parents understand that fact and do not try to act as if their child-rearing task is as easy as it might otherwise be. If they understand that their situation is inherently very difficult, they'll be much better off than if they ignore that fact.

A final note on this subject concerns the frequency with which people notice a return to babylike behavior on the part of two- to three-and-a-half-year-old children when there is a crawling baby in the home. Often when people ask about the meaning of a return to bedwetting or soiled diapers or very little interest in age mates or resurfacing of baby talk or sleeping problems, they don't mention the fact that there is a younger child at home. It's as if they are so concerned with the older one that they don't recognize that the presence of the younger child has anything to do with the older child's problems.

In many of these cases, in my experience, there is a younger child at home. Even though the symptoms the older child is showing may be quite diverse, the underlying cause of this regression is the presence of the younger child and the displacement felt by the older one. Often the treatment outlined above, which is built on an awareness of the natural sensitivities of the older child, does make a difference for the better.

Helping Children Cope with Divorce

Michelle is a totally silent underweight infant of five months. Lying quietly in the crib, she turns her pasty white face away from the activity in the room. Her new foster sister promptly nicknames her Casper the Ghost and sets about winning her attention, not very successfully.

Michelle's father walked out of her life the day she was born, and her distracted, financially harassed mother has had no energy or attention to give her infant daughter while she struggled to deal with her own disrupted life.

Johnny is a merry, talkative six-year-old. He matter-of-factly explains to his kindergarten teacher that he needs two papers to take home, one for Mother and one to save for Daddy, whom he visits each weekend.

A classmate overhears and is reminded that he has heard the unfamiliar word *divorce* in connection with Johnny. He asks a question and gets a simple answer: "That means my Mother and Daddy don't live together, but of course he's still my Daddy." Two papers in hand, he follows his classmates out of the door with a good-bye wave for teacher.

There has been a steady rise in the rate of divorce in American families. Almost everyone knows a young relative, neighbor's child, or school car pool rider who is experiencing the separation of his or her parents. While a great deal of work has been done to help adults learn about and cope positively with the stresses of divorce, until recently research into its effects on children was scanty and not very helpful.

Now there is a growing body of information about children and divorce—how it affects them, how they cope, and how adults can help. This chapter will summarize some of this information and suggest some positive things you can do.

THE PRINCIPAL EFFECTS OF DIVORCE ON CHILDREN

As Michelle and Johnny illustrate, no single description fits all the children experienceing divorce. How the child was doing before the divorce, the age of the child, the kind of help adults are giving, and other factors help create the picture. To make the description easier we will divide children by age and discuss the methods they use to cope. The studies seem to show that effects on the child are related to his or her developmental stage.

Birth to Two Years

The child from birth to two years cannot label her experiences with words, but divorce means fundamental changes in her life. She will sense distraction or emotional turmoil in the parent. If one parent leaves her daily life, she will feel that loss and be distressed, even though that distress may be wordless. Even very young children separated from parents feel grief, loss, and pain.

Most children in this age group can readily accept a substitute caregiver to provide warmth and closeness, but a stable parenting figure with time and emotional warmth to give the child is urgently needed. Very short periods when a parent is absent (a week or two) are experienced as total loss by the very young child.

The less the child is able to understand, the more temper-amentally fearful he is; the less his responses seem to affect what happens to him (i.e., his crying doesn't prevent the parent from leaving or bring the parent back), the more upset the child may be. This may be reflected in loss of appetite, respiratory upsets, excessive crying, or withdrawal into silence and apathy.

Preschool

The preschool child reacts to divorce with noticeable changes in behavior. Toilet training may relapse, bad dreams are common, and there may be much crying and whining. She may be afraid to be left with baby-sitters or at school. She often becomes very possessive of toys and attached to objects of one sort or another. Many children are preoccupied with being "good," believing that their "badness" caused the divorce and that being "good" will bring their parents together again. All these behaviors are more pronounced when the parents' divorce was sudden and unexplained.

Preschoolers also use fantasy. They may talk to an imaginary parent or pretend to sleep with him or her. There are often threatening animals in the pretend world of these children.

More than half of the children in this age group are doing worse at the end of the first year after divorce than immediately following the separation of the parents. This seems to be especially true for children whose parents are still feeling hurt, rage, and humiliation and are inconsistent in caring for, disciplining, and showing affection for their preschoolers.

Five and Six

The five- or six-year-old child responds to divorce with frequent expressions of longing for his absent parent and with hopes for reconciliation. Because the child is often restless, distractible, and daydreaming, schoolwork tends to be poor. This child is apt to get along poorly with other children his age and to cling to adults. He may become very depressed. Often children this age deny the whole divorce situation or blame themselves even when given contrary explanations.

Seven and Eight

Children age seven to eight react to divorce in a markedly different way from children in any other age group. These children often show extreme, open suffering and may be almost unable to keep going. They are not able to use fantasy to deny the situation as the younger child may do, and they do not have the maturity or independence to cope by using distance to get away from the pain of their situation, as an older child will. The child of this age is especially vulnerable to the crisis of divorce.

Nine and Older

The older child copes by distancing himself from his family.

He actually separates himself physically from the situation.

Beginning at about age nine, the child is able to act on his own and has a circle of interests and friends outside the family, so he turns to them with increased intensity. He removes himself from the divorce by becoming more involved with his peer group and with school, sports, or other activities—which is a normal trend, anyway, at this developmental stage. An effective parenting response is to encourage the child to engage in these activities.

WHAT KINDS OF HELP WORK BEST?

Couples who are divorcing are experiencing a great deal of emotional stress and change, and their ability to parent may suffer during this period. They should receive some counseling that is specifically child-centered. That is, it should help them be aware of their child's behaviors and include suggestions to deal with these behaviors constructively.

Counseling is needed most urgently in the divorce when everything is more disorganized. Adults benefit from having someone to help them sort out the job of being a parent from the job of being a spouse.

Frequent contact with the noncustodial parent helps the child adjust, even if the parent/child relationship was poor before the divorce. However, the custodial parent should not try to make these visits a source of fighting or a test of loyalty. Children of all ages need constant reassurance that both parents will continue to love, care for, and protect them. There may be an unspoken question: "If you can stop loving one another, will you at some time also stop loving me?"

In addition to these general suggestions, specific help is needed by each age group.

Over Nine

The parents should be encouraged to let the child be independent. It's hard on the child when an overburdened parent shifts too much of the decision-making care of younger children, household work, or companionship responsibility from the absent spouse to the child.

Friends can assist with these adult responsibilities by providing transportation or other assistance. Letting a divorcing mother out of car pool responsibilities for a semester, for instance, may be one of the best things a friend can do for the whole family.

Though seeing the absent parent is important to the child, very often custodial parents find that the older child does not want to have his activities disrupted by visiting arrangements. Then it will be up to the noncustodial parent to make some effort to go where his child is (watch him play basketball, go to her track meet, take a turn at the parents' hot dog stand on music contest day) in order to maintain contact. Friends can make this easier by including the child and his noncustodial parent in family outings or a summer barbecue or by inviting that parent to accompany them to school affairs or community activities involving their children.

While older children heavily use peer group support, some also welcome adult friendships and may respond to low-key overtures. Some will use the parents of a friend as a sort of backup family, though they will probably be willing to come only under the guise of visiting the friend. Occasionally, an older child shows enough difficulty in adjusting that getting some individual counseling is a good idea.

Seven or Eight

The child in this age group is apt to suffer more if people try to talk about the divorce directly with her. Some child counselors instead use a tactic they call *divorce monologue,* in which the therapist tells how "some seven- and eight-year-olds feel about divorce." This often helps the child feel less lonely and more confident.

Sometimes children express concern about specific problems of their parents. Counselors who work with children find that it is best to be firm in telling children that they must leave adult problems to adults to solve, and this seems to reassure the child.

Adult friends who are close to the child might talk with the child in this way.

Children in this age group do best when they have easy, frequent access to noncustodial parents. When parents are out for revenge or use the children as weapons, the children suffer.

Friends can help adults accept the child's need for his absent parent and assist in the logistics of the contacts.

Five and Six

Since the child in this age group shows his distress through his behaviors, he can be helped by trying to see what is triggering specific behaviors and by improving verbal communication. Parents must frequently reassure him, in words, that they will continue to love, care for, and protect the child.

The parent may also need to learn how to put the child's feelings into words for her—for instance, "If I were a little girl, and my Daddy went away, I might worry that my Mommy would go away, too. Do you feel that way sometimes?" Following such a conversation, the parent should reaffirm continuing love.

Child therapists have learned that behaviors of the parent that are worrying or upsetting to the child can be pointed out to the parent.

These include making the child feel torn between loyalties, complaining, and discussing worries about finances. The child may take very literally such overstatements as "I guess we're all just supposed to starve," and "I don't know how we'll manage to get you kids clothes for school." Sometimes a close friend can ease things a great deal by listening to these complaints or worries on an adult level and at the same time help the parent remember not to burden a small child with them.

Some changes in parental behavior will lessen the clinging and whiny, irritable behavior. It may help if the parent structures each day to give some undivided attention to the child. Frequent visits with the absent parent need to be encouraged. Grandparents, neighbors, teachers, and others can supplement the time parents are able to give the child.

Preschool

As with the five- and six-year-olds, the help given to the preschool child needs to center on the child/parent relationship. The children who have the most difficulty are those whose custodial parents are still angry, hurt, or confused and who talk and complain about their situation in front of the children. If visiting is allowed at all, they frequently sabotage the visits or make the child feel guilty about them.

Parents may be able to eliminate these behaviors by talking them out with other adults. It's necessary to sort out the spouse relationship, which is now dissolved, from the parent relationship, which is still going on. Consistent, firm discipline is needed acutely, especially when a preschool boy is living with his mother. Preschoolers should get repeated and constant assurance of the love of both parents. They may also need to be reminded gently that a reconciliation is not possible.

Birth to Two Years

The child of this age cannot ask questions or understand explanations on a subject as complicated as divorce, any more than the very young adopted child understands the vocabulary of adoption. The words should be used and the explanation given, but the bulk of the necessary help will come in the form of adult attempts to understand the child's needs and provide for them.

The child must have his time frame respected. In a very short time the absent parent will be a stranger. This means that visits must be very frequent. It means that the adult must be willing to wait and let the child "look him over" when he comes to visit, rather than rush in with hugs and kisses.

The child needs to have his emotional immaturity respected. While he cannot understand, he does feel the tension, distraction, grief, or anger of the parent caring for him. Adults need to respond to the child with lots of attention, smiling back as he smiles, returning affectionate overtures, being aware of the child's presence.

On the other hand, the child cannot serve as a focus for all the love, longing, or need for comfort that an adult who has lost a partner may be feeling. He is a child and cannot be a substitute for his absent parent, nor should he be the focus of anger or resentment toward that parent. Because he is so vulnerable, adults around him must take care to offer loving protection against unfair adult emotional demands.

For the very young child one change is enough. There will be less anxiety and distress about the loss of a parent if the rest of her world stays the same. This means that a friend who offers to baby-sit should try to do so in the child's own home. If Mother must now go to work, the best child care arrangement will be one that means as little other change as possible. Siblings should be available, and sleeping arrangements, toys, schedules, and other factors in her environment should be disrupted as little as possible. Changes should be gradual and made at a rate at which she can absorb them.

Children from birth to age two need a responsive, nurturing caregiver for their social development. Decent physical care is not enough—it must be provided by someone who knows how to nurture the child's spirit. In spite of the pain and distraction of dealing with divorce, the parents must consistently provide this themselves or secure a principal caregiver who can do this during the divorce crisis. The child should not be left to wait it out for better days.

ADULTS OUTSIDE THE DIVORCE SITUATION

In spite of the evidence that all children should receive specific, timely, and age-appropriate facts about their parents' divorce, 80 percent of all children under five years of age are not told why their absent parent left home. An adult who has friends or family members who are divorcing can help the child by encouraging the parents to tell the child the facts.

This may be difficult, and it is often avoided because it makes the situation so final to one or both parents that they don't want to do it. But the child needs this information. Specifically, he needs to have his parents tell him about the divorce, that there will be no reconciliation (where this is the case, of course), that the divorce is not the child's fault, that both parents still love him, and that he will not be left alone but rather protected and cared for. He needs information and assurances repeatedly, especially at younger ages.

Even if the child received information and support at the time of the divorce, he may need additional help a year or two later. Sometimes the pain of a divorce goes on in adult lives for months, and the parents may be too preoccupied with their own feelings to be aware of the misery or difficulty the child is experiencing. Again, adult friends can be aware of the child's needs and carefully and sensitively help the parent see the situation.

If there is guilt left over in adult minds, it may be especially hard to admit that the child is having difficulty because of the divorce. The friend can, for instance, find the right kind of counseling and provide baby-sitting, transportation, or whatever else may be needed. The parent may also need encouragement to secure counseling for the child.

Since it is harmful for children of any age to be used as a vent for negative emotions, parents need their own friends who are willing to listen. This listening is often not pleasant, and we may wish to cut off the conversation or avoid a divorcing friend "until the worst is over." Willingness to listen, to avoid judging, and to help in practical ways through the transition period involve genuine caring. Indirectly, it will also help the child.

In spite of good intentions, most adults who divorce have a great deal of trouble separating their feelings about a former marriage partner from their feelings about that partner's share in raising their children. They need help and encouragement to arrive at good custody or visiting arrangements. Friends who can listen are invaluable in this process.

Adults who care about children recognize the consequences of divorce for children. In an effort to be encouraging and supportive to the grown-ups, there has been a tendency to overlook the children. Research indicates, however, that divorce has disorganizing and potentially bad effects on them, too. A year or two is a long time in the life of a child, even if he recovers at the end of that time. He needs to minimize the hurt. Probably the most urgent need is for education of the divorcing parents themselves in the needs of their children—often best received through a supportive friend.

Divorce is a crisis for children. All of the adults in a community can play a role in helping children meet that crisis and keep growing.

Moving On . . . with Children

One in five American families moves each year, sometimes across the country. How do the children of these families respond to the changes moving brings? How can parents help their children deal effectively with these changes?

For years child development professionals have debated the pros and cons of moving versus letting the child grow up in one community. But often families must move regardless of the effect on children. In those circumstances, what can parents do to help children make the most of their changing situation and ensure a positive, growth-producing experience?

This chapter is an attempt to accept moving as one of the events that happens in a child's life and to offer some suggestions to minimize the bad aspects of it and maximize the good ones.

You can be so busy dealing with your own emotions and plans that you may not realize that the things that make moving difficult for adults are operating for the child, too. Let's spell out some feelings that children may have.

114

LOSING CONTROL

Moving may be difficult for the child because he feels a loss of control over his life. Depending on his age, a child takes for granted the stability of the environment around him and begins to make plans. Having learned the hazards of his neighborhood, he develops strategies for handling them. For instance, in our neighborhood there is a dog that always lunges out and barks at passersby. But our children have learned that he is on a chain, and they routinely cross his path on the other side of the alley, a safe distance from the end of the chain.

A child learns from other children the characteristics of the teacher she will have next year and has an idea of the behavior necessary to meet the teacher's standards. Your daughter knows the age rules of the local softball league and the hours of the library and stores. Knowing all these facts and hundreds more, the child plans her life around them and feels a sense of control.

When the family moves, everything becomes an unknown. Even a very independent and carefree child will experience anxiety about new circumstances. A worrier may spend a great many hours fretting about relatively minor (from an adult point of view) details. After years of being encouraged to be independent and responsible, a child may feel that "they" are taking the foundations out from under his plans. Both children who have moved a lot and children who have never moved may experience the process of moving as a loss of control that produces anxiety.

"WHAT I WANT DOESN'T MATTER"

The child may be upset by moving because it upsets the nature of his universe. While most homes do not revolve around the child's needs, that is the way the child sees the world. Growing up is, in some measure, the process of going from being totally egocentric (the nursing child assumes that the world exists to satisfy his need) to engaging in mutually satisfying give and take with all the other people he knows. Since a family move is almost never made because that is what the child wants, he may quite suddenly have to learn to cope with a situation in which his wants don't rule the family. Because the young child thinks in black-and-white terms, he may translate this into "What I want doesn't matter at all" and be very hurt or angry about the move.

Your child may be upset by a planned move because she realizes it means a lot of unknowns or because she feels incompetent to handle the new situation. Most of us let our lives drift into ruts where we don't have to work to the maximum of our ability to have a fairly comfortable life, and children do the same. Like adults, the child may take friendships for granted and learn the shortcuts to getting work done.

Moving disrupts this complacency, and the child may tend to resist the changes he sees ahead, especially if he is not sure of his ability to handle them. Some children make new friends easily; others do not. Some children welcome exploring a new environment; to others it is full of hidden dangers. The unknowns ahead and the characteristics of a particular child interact to affect how he sees the move.

LEAVING FAMILIAR FACES BEHIND

Your children may resist moving because they regret the loss of the familiar and beloved. All of us develop attachments for our surroundings, though the depth of these attachments varies, of course. We miss the friendly face at the corner gas station, the big maples that shaded our street, the sunset over a familiar horizon, the sounds and smells of waking up in a known place. They are part of our roots, and pulling them up is painful. With our heads we know that we will learn to love the place we are going, but our emotions are tied to the place where we have been. We love it, and loss brings pain and emptiness.

The very young child experiences loss as absolutely total. The statement "You will see her again someday" has almost no meaning when a friend is being left behind. The school-aged child may believe you but isn't good at waiting. The older child is realistic enough to know that occasional visits do not bring the same satisfaction—that, in a sense, "you can't go home again." For all the family, moving does mean painful loss.

Having described some ways in which the child may respond negatively to the idea of moving, let's discuss some things the family can do to help.

SOME THINGS STAY THE SAME

When a child feels a loss of control, there are several ways you can respond. The child may be able to understand that he will still be in charge of many things in his life. You are moving as a family, and the family rules and ways of doing things will stay the same. Give him concrete examples of the kinds of ways in which he will remain in charge.

You may also want to talk to your child about the fact that not even adults are in control of everything. If she is upset at your power to control her, it may help her to realize that you too can have your life upset—that this is a condition of being human. A sense of our place in the scheme of the universe helps us deal with events beyond our control. People die, crops fail for lack of rain, friends diappoint us. In the context of moving, the child can begin to learn to accept things he cannot control and to learn that all of us—parents and children—must do this.

BEGIN DISCUSSIONS EARLY

We've said that moving upsets the child's universe. In the rush of decision making associated with moving, parents may overlook the need to talk with the child about the reasons for this move. Even very young children can understand a great deal that is told to them in simple language. It is probably better to overestimate than to underestimate how much your child can grasp. You can imagine how you would react if your spouse came home one day and said, "The moving company will be here to take us to Upper Mongolia next Tuesday." This may be about the way this move is striking your child. He may not completely understand Dad's excitement over a new job opportunity, the dead-end nature of Mother's present job, or the need to be closer to an ailing grandmother, but he should hear these situations explained. The factors that are leading you to decide that this is a good move for your family should be communicated to the child.

Let the child give you her objections, too. If possible, children should be involved while it is still possible to say, "We are thinking of moving. What do you think?" If there is really no choice involved for you either, your children need to know that. You cannot expect them to understand until the facts are known. In the process of deciding to move, the family's values and priorities can be clarified in a way that will be helpful to all. If the discussions with the children begin early in the process, you may even decide not to move as you become aware of your real values.

INTRODUCE SOME NEW SITUATIONS

Your child may be upset because he feels he will not be able to handle the unknowns. One of the ways you can meet this emotion is to provide realistic introductions to some of the new situations involved. It may be possible for you to introduce him to the new area before he moves there. Recently we drove with the children to what will be our new home. We showed them the rooms they will live in and talked about where their existing furniture might fit. We brought home floor plans so they could continue to work on arranging their new rooms.

We took our eleven-year-old boy to his new school on a day when there happened to be a rummage sale. He explored the building and grounds, glanced at some of the textbooks, and checked out the gymnasium. He asked questions of the people working around the school and found a boy who could answer some questions, such as, "What happens when you're tardy?" and "When does soccer practice start?" We did not know what questions he might have, but the chance to explore on his own gave him an opportunity to get some of the answers he wanted.

It is not always possible to make such a trip, but usually you can get a great deal of information if you look at it as needed from the child's point of view. A map with house, school playgrounds, and swimming pool marked on it might permit him to draw a route to them from your new house. Perhaps you could get picture postcards of significant buildings. Our son has delighted in wearing a sweat shirt from what will be his sister's new school. We took him to Sunday School there, and he met some children his age.

Acquaintances in the new town took him for a whole day at their home and then to a volunteer fire department carnival with their children that night. He looks forward to going to that carnival next year as a resident. Perhaps you could arrange for a pen pal to write to your child and answer questions by mail. As she knows what the new situation will require, she will develop confidence that she can handle it or strategies and skills to get ready to handle it. You can provide the facts she needs and the emotional support and suggestions.

Listen for disguised questions and fears. Jeff has a beloved dog, Duster, and as he surveyed the new territory he apparently began to wonder if Duster could handle it. But he did not directly express his fears. Two years ago when a friend of his moved their family dog was unable to adjust to the new home and died.

Out of the blue Jeff asked us recently, "How come Penny died when they had to move her?" In the conversation that followed we were able to discuss Jeff's worry about Duster and reassure him that Duster would be able to make the change.

As you are able to meet your fears, talk about them, and plan ways to overcome them, your child will copy these behaviors. If you talk about the challenges and opportunities and set about learning the skills you need, your child will be more optimistic and anticipate the changes, too.

HELPING YOUR CHILD WITH THE LOSS OF THE LOVED AND FAMILIAR

Approach the loss of the familiar in moving in the same way you would help your child accept the death of a pet or the loss of a beloved toy. Although this loss is more general, children should be allowed to express grief, to be angry about moving and have that anger channeled into nondestructive actions, to feel that you share the sadness. It will take time to work through the grieving, and you should not expect instant acceptance or even steady progress toward acceptance of the loss. Some days your child may seem quite reconciled to moving and even eager for the challenge. Other days he may feel quite sad and blue and be unable to think of anything nice about moving.

It may be possible to provide for transition objects and behaviors. I have since regretted that one time when we were moving I pressured our two older children into giving up toys they had not played with much for the last year or so. I did not know then that children often regress to earlier behaviors and that having those objects would help them make the move. Be sure to let your child take along into the new home beloved possessions (within reason!), even those you see no need for. It is not a good time to ask your child to give them up.

Your child might enjoy taking pictures of people and places

she is leaving. A younger child could suggest the pictures, and you could spend the morning taking pictures and then picnic in a favorite park together. If pictures are already available, perhaps you could work together to make a scrapbook of her favorite people and places to take along to the new home.

It is a good idea to arrange to have a physical examination and dental checkup with familiar doctors before you go. This may allow you to avoid an emergency trip to brand-new professionals soon after arrival in the new place and will provide up-to-date records to take along.

Avoid adding unnecessary pressures to the child's life while you are making a change in residence. You may even need to let down standards temporarily as the child deals with the stress of moving. However, familiar schedules and structures will help him make the change in physical environment, so don't go overboard and let the child "get away with murder." It will actually make the move more difficult for all of you.

Try to be sure that your child gets enough rest, eats regular meals, keeps up piano lessons, etc., as much as possible. But don't be too surprised or upset if your child's appetite is temporarily poor or if there are toilet accidents or bad dreams. Your children will probably return to normal behavior soon after settling into the new home.

Change is a part of human life. Moving to a new home means many changes, and as you help your child handle them you will be providing valuable practice for making other kinds of changes in life.

The Story of Phillip

Phillip was a bright, active boy.

His upbringing provided him with love and attention, good nutrition, and plenty of learning experiences in a traditional family situation.

After Phillip entered school, however, he was no longer a smiling, carefree child. In the classroom his attention frequently wandered, and he was unable to follow directions or stay with a task until it was completed. There were fights at school and quarrels at home.

Unfortunately, this is a familiar story for many American families. But this particular one has a happy ending.

Phillip's parents happened to mention the problems he was having to a professional educator and, consequently, Phillip was tested and evaluated. The results indicated that Phillip's general functioning level was approximately at what would normally be expected for a child his age. However, he did have particular difficulty in tasks (such as the "three Rs") that required space-time sequencing and stable visual perception.

Phillip was enrolled in a special remedial learning program to help fill in the gaps in his childhood learning experiences. Today the changes are apparent—he is a National Honor Society student and has attained Dean's List honors at his university.

If Phillip's parents had known when he was small what they knew at the conclusion of his training program, he probably wouldn't have had those learning problems. His parents were concerned that other

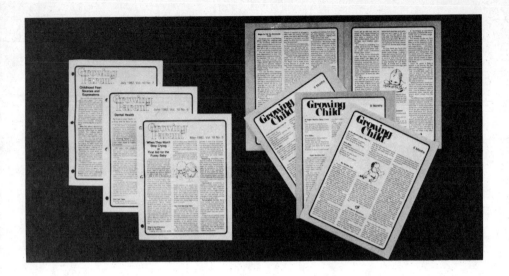

children were having the same problems—problems that didn't have to happen.

His father, Dennis Dunn, was in the publishing business. It was a logical step to develop a monthly newsletter to help other parents.

Mr. Dunn engaged child development experts from across the country to write the newsletter to tell parents all about early childhood development, how to ensure that proper development takes place, why early learning experiences are important for future learning, and much more.

The newsletter, *Growing Child,* now covers the first six years of growth and has touched the lives of many thousands of children and their parents. A companion publication, *Growing Parent,* was a logical next step.

Growing Parent is a monthly supplement to *Growing Child* that talks about the special problems and pressures of parenthood. It helps parents know themselves, understand others, and cope with the reality of living.

Growing Child also offers an entire line of age-graded developmental toys, books, and records.

Bridging the gap from one small boy to many thousands of children wasn't just an idle dream—the people at *Growing Child* made that dream a reality.

For more information and a free sample issue of *Growing Child,* send your child's birth date (or expected date) along with your name and address to:

22 North Second Street
Post Office Box 620
Department GPB
Lafayette, IN 47902